RAVEL
LE TOMBEAU DE COUPERIN FOR THE PIANO
EDITED BY NANCY BRICARD

Contents

This edition is dedicated to my beloved husband, Sherwyn M. Woods, M.D., whose continued love, support and encouragement made the production of these editions possible.

Nancy Bricard

Second Edition

Cover art: Rue du Mont-Cenis, 1914
by Maurice Utrillo (French, 1883–1955)
Giraudon / Art Resource, New York

Foreword

ABOUT THIS EDITION

Le Tombeau de Couperin is unique in that it is Ravel's first published post-World War I composition and the austere harmonic style reflects a distinct change from the rich textures of his pre-war compositions. This critical edition should be of value to teachers, students and performing artists as it addresses in-depth matters of tempo, fingering, pedaling, translation and printing errors as well as stylistic considerations. Some of the material in the sections on **Style**, **Interpretation**, and **Technique** are taken from my previous publications of other masterworks of Maurice Ravel, *Gaspard de la Nuit*[1] and *Miroirs*,[2] with modifications appropriate for *Le Tombeau de Couperin.*

Ravel began composing *Le Tombeau de Couperin* in 1914 and completed the work in 1917. It was published in 1918 by Durand et Cie.[3] The autograph is in the private collection of Madame Alexandre Taverne of Monte Carlo, Monaco and consists of 18 pages signed and dated July 1914 and June–November 1917. The first performance was given on April 11, 1919 by Marguerite Long in Salle Gaveau, Paris.

Unfortunately, for the first printing of the Alfred Masterwork edition of *Le Tombeau de Couperin*, all attempts to contact Madame Taverne (owner of the autograph) for the purpose of consulting and studying the autograph were unsuccessful. However, the original sketches and drafts are located at the Pierpont Morgan Library in New York City and, thanks to the generous help of Mr. J. Rigbie Turner, Mary Flagler Cary Curator of Music Manuscripts and Books, I was able to study photocopies of these drafts and sketches. They were of immense value. Since that time, an individual, who wishes to remain anonymous, has provided me with a photocopy of Ravel's autograph manuscript.

The first printing of this edition was based on one of the earliest engraved editions as well as three subsequent reprints. All these reprints were issued by the original publisher, Durand et Cie, with no additional corrections or changes in any of them. A few omissions occurred, however, probably caused by the age and wear of the plates used for engraving. These omissions are mentioned in the footnotes as they appear in the score. After an in-depth study and comparison of the autograph to the first printings of *Le Tombeau de Couperin*, I have found very few differences between them. When any contradictions do occur, they are mentioned in this second and subsequent printings.

There are very few errors to be found in the original edition of *Le Tombeau de Couperin* in contrast to the multiple errors existing in

1 Nancy Bricard (Ed.), *Ravel: Gaspard de la Nuit* (Van Nuys: Alfred Publishing Company, 1990).

2 Nancy Bricard (Ed.), *Ravel: Miroirs* (Van Nuys: Alfred Publishing Company, 1993).

3 Maurice Ravel, *Le Tombeau de Couperin* (Paris: Durand et Cie, 1918).

Ravel's piano and portrait of his mother by Luc-Albert Moreau

the original editions of *Gaspard de la Nuit* and *Miroirs.* The errors that do exist in *Le Tombeau de Couperin* have all been corrected by the editor in this new edition and the source or justification for these corrections is footnoted on the same page. Footnote comments are also used to clarify certain notes or signs that are confusing as originally notated. Notes, signs or symbols (such as warning accidentals) that have been omitted by mistake from the original edition are found in parentheses where they are missing. I have used this format not only for the purpose of clarity, but also because of the pedagogical principle that a correct first reading of the score is exceedingly important. This first reading makes a lasting auditory and haptic impression that is needlessly difficult to change. All tempos, dynamics, interpretive remarks and right-/left-hand indications that appear in French belong to Ravel. English translations can be found for French terms only when they first appear in each piece. All metronome marks are Ravel's with the exception of the Rigaudon marking, which is editorial. Although they do not appear in the autograph, they were most likely added by Ravel in the first printing of the Durand edition. The French spelling of the word *menuet* instead of *minuet* is used throughout this publication since that is how it appears in Ravel's score.

Information regarding printing errors and Ravel's interpretive wishes come from the noted French pianists and pedagogues: Robert Casadesus (1899–1972), Vlado Perlemuter (b. 1904), Marguerite Long (1874–1966) and Marcel Ciampi (1891–1980), my former professor in France. Casadesus, Perlemuter, and Long knew the composer well and were major interpreters of his works. Casadesus and Perlemuter recorded the complete works of Ravel, the former on the Columbia Masterworks label and the latter on the Pathé Vox label.

Ravel made few pedal indications, and these appear in the score as: 𝆮 (damper pedal); 𝆯 (release of the damper pedal); une corde (one string—una corda pedal); 3 cordes (three strings—release the una corda pedal) and *sourdine* (una corda). All other pedal marks are editorial.

The autograph and the Durand editions have no fingering and there are only three hand indications. These are the *m.g.* (*main gauche:* left hand) indication in measure 27 of the Fugue and the *m.g., m.d.* (*main droite:* right hand) indications in measure 34 of the Fugue. These indications are identified in the footnotes. I have added many *divisi* and fingerings not only to aid in the technical and interpretive aspects of the music, but also to facilitate difficult passages for pianists with small hands. Alternate fingerings are also given and are separated by a horizontal line or illustrated in the footnotes. It is often helpful first to practice a passage with the given fingerings until it can be played up to tempo. Some fingerings work very well at a slow tempo, but not at the actual tempo of the piece. If a fingering does not seem to work at tempo, one should try the alternate fingerings and *divisi.* As a matter of personal preference, I almost always change fingers when repeating expressive notes such as the repeated notes found in the melodic lines of the Menuet (see measures 1, 9, 25, and 29). These notes should vary in nuance and I feel that varying the fingers helps to produce these shades of difference. This opinion, however, is not shared by all pianists. Many prefer using the same finger on repeated expressive notes for the purpose of developing finger sensitivity and maintaining maximum control. Changing from one finger to another (finger substitution) on a note is marked, for example, as 3–5. Numbers are circled to indicate using more than one finger on a note, as in measure 51 of the Toccata: ㉜ . I often use multiple fingers on a single note as I feel it not only facilitates the production of a different kind of sound but also aids in isolating a note to give it the intended character.

The Piano Music of Ravel

STYLE

The essence of Ravel's genius was a supremely intelligent way of looking at things, whether the most passionate or the most pathetic, and subjecting them to the discipline of style.[4]

(From a eulogy delivered by Jean Zay, French Minister of Education, at the funeral of Ravel)

The art of Ravel passed through a wide range of differing styles and periods. One can easily identify the Baroque, Classical and jazz elements in his compositions. However, in spite of this diversification, all his music possesses a unique personal touch that is distinguished by exquisite grace and elegance.

4 Arbie Orenstein, *Ravel: Man and Musician* (New York: Columbia University Press, 1968), 108–109.

Ravel, born in 1875, was influenced by the ideas and philosophies that developed at the end of the Franco-Prussian War (1870–71). Friedrich Nietzsche (1844–1900) observed that this war seemed to have unleashed France's creative spirit. French art, literature and music assumed the lead over previous German domination. There was an integration of the arts as painters, writers and musicians came together to freely exchange views. Paris became the cultural capital of Europe and France took a prominent position of leadership in the world of music. This musical renaissance was marked by the development of the concept of music as a purely sonorous art for its own sake rather than as a means of personal expression. This was in direct contrast to the subjective style of the 19th-century Romantic movement, which had placed emphasis on individual feelings and emotions. Ravel was certainly receptive and responsive to this change. He felt that technical mastery of his craft was of more importance and value than the expression of personal feelings, and that inspiration resulted from a relentless pursuit of technical excellence. He often quoted the poet Charles Baudelaire's (1821–67) statement: "Inspiration is decidedly the sister of daily work." Ravel criticized those who claimed that their music was sincere, but who wrote imperfect works. He said:

> Sincerity is of no value unless one's conscience helps to make it apparent. This conscience compels us to turn ourselves into good craftsmen. My objective, therefore, is technical perfection. I can strive unceasingly to this end, since I am certain of never being able to attain it. The important thing is to get nearer to it all the time.[5]

Igor Stravinsky called Ravel the "Swiss clock maker" because of his extraordinary craftsmanship. There is no impulsive quality to his music. Instead, one finds precision, attention to detail, inventiveness, imagination and sensuous refinement. His work is methodical and well conceived. Each note and phrase is in its place of importance. Émile Vuillermoz (1878–1960), a prominent critic and lifelong friend of Ravel stated:

> One can well see Maurice Ravel leaning on his bench, the loupe in his eye, inserting a note in one of his orchestra scores with the same care of a good worker fixing a ruby in the mechanism of a watch. That precision, that meticulousness, and that dexterity of hand are all to his honor.[6]

Colette (1873–1954), the great French writer, described Ravel as being "excessively shy, aloof in bearing and sober in conversation."[7] This reserve is often found in his music. It has the character of restraint, not abandon. This is not to say, however, that his music is devoid of emotional content or impact. Ravel himself said:

> Great music must always come from the heart. Music that is made only with technique and intellect is not worth the paper it is written on.[8]

Ravel communicates his ideas by means of nuance, form and color. His colors, however, are generally more articulated and detached than those of Debussy, which tend to be more homogenized. Ravel's fascination with piano sonorities led him to look beyond the known capacity of the instrument and to experiment with new ways of extending its ability to produce pianistic sound effects and instrumental colors. This imagination in the conception of sound textures is prevalent in all his music.

"The dance," writes M. André Suares, "governs all the music of Ravel like that of the Spanish and the harpsichordists."[9] Ravel had a predilection for stylized dance rhythms and it pleased him to use forms such as Menuet, Pavane, Forlane, Rigaudon, Habanera, and waltzes of all varieties. Melody also is an essential element in his music. He was taught this by André Gédalge (1856–1926), who told all his pupils "Whatever sauce you put around the melody is a matter of taste, what is important is the melodic line and this doesn't vary."[10] Roland-Manuel (pen name of Alexis Manuel Lévy) was a Belgian musicologist, critic, and one of Ravel's students. He describes Ravel's melodic lyricism as "supple, but extremely pure, with contours which strongly indicate something Italian, in the sense of the Italianism of Mozart, Schubert, even of Weber or of Chopin."[11]

Another feature of Ravel's piano music was its virtuoso quality. This stems directly from the keyboard traditions of Chopin, Liszt and Saint-Saëns. Walter Gieseking felt that "Scarbo" (*Gaspard de la Nuit*) and "Alborada del gracioso" (*Miroirs*), in addition to being among the most difficult piano works ever written, were musical masterpieces:

> The right expression is so important, because these intricate pianistic acrobatics are never deprived of musical sense, of artistic value. . . . It is always real music, which one may call refined, concentrated, perhaps even too sophisticated, but it is written primarily to create beautiful, enchanting, expressive piano sonorities, and if this music is technically very complex, it is nevertheless based on musically perfectly logical conceptions.[12]

Although Ravel forged new paths in his growth as a composer, he always retained his ties to tradition and worked within its framework. During his tour in the United States (1927–28), in an interview with the musicologist David Ewen, for the music journal *Étude*, Ravel said:

> I am not a modern composer in the strictest sense of the word, because my music is an evolution, not a revolution. While I have always been receptive to new ideas in music, I have never tried to throw the laws of harmony and composition into the discard. On the contrary, I have always drawn inspiration generously

5 Roland-Manuel, "Lettres de Maurice Ravel et documents inédits," *Revue de Musicologie*, XXXVIII (Paris, July 1956).

6 Émile Vuillermoz et al., *Maurice Ravel par quelques-uns de ses familiers* (Paris: Éditions du Tambourinaire, 1939), 13.

7 H. H. Stuckenschmidt, *Maurice Ravel*, trans. Samuel R. Rosenbaum (Philadelphia: Chilton Book Company, 1968), 47.

8 Stuckenschmidt, 224.

9 Roland-Manuel, *Ravel* (Paris: Librairie Gallimard, 1948), 158.

10 Orenstein, 131.

11 Ibid., 132.

12 Ibid., 136.

> from the masters. I have never stopped studying Mozart. To the greatest extent possible my music is built up on the traditions of the past and grows out of them. . . .[13]

These convictions were further clarified by Ravel during a conversation with the pianist and composer Manuel Rosenthal (b. 1904), who asked Ravel if he could explain the difference between evolution and revolution. The anecdote that follows was his answer:

> Suppose you are in a room, studying . . .; after a few hours you feel that the atmosphere is a little stuffy and you need to change the air, and you open the window. You let the fresh air enter the room, after a while you close the window, that's all. That's evolution. You are in the room and you feel that you need a change of air, and you take a stone, put that through the window and break the window. Of course the fresh air enters, but after that you have to repair the window. That's revolution! . . . I don't see myself needing to break a window; I know how to open it![14]

INTERPRETATION

Do not interpret my music, just play it![15]
(Maurice Ravel)

Throughout his career, Ravel was frequently called upon to interpret his music, both in the concert hall and on recordings. Anyone who has heard these performances will attest to the fact that he was not a good performer of his own music. Émile Vuillermoz protested against the habit of bringing a composer before the public in a role that he was incapable of filling. "M. Ravel is continually brought out as a pianist or as a conductor, whilst he cannot possibly shine in either of these two specialties."[16]

Nevertheless, Ravel was adamant with others about the interpretation of his music when dealing with other performers. Hélène Jourdan-Morhange (1888–1961), a violinist to whom Ravel dedicated his *Sonata for Violin and Piano*, said that she never knew a composer so sure of himself with regard to indications marked in his music. "Ravel said not only everything that one must do, but above all everything one must not do."[17] For example, he had such a horror of pianists making ritards that he continually wrote *sans ralentir* (without ritard) in the score. Ravel's focus on every minute detail concerning the performance of his music was probably a reaction against the excesses of Romantic license practiced by so many of the virtuosos of the day. It was these excesses and other undisciplined exaggerations in the field of the arts that prompted the famous writer André Gide (1869–1951) to say, "Art is born out of constraint, lives from struggle, dies from liberty."[18]

Émile Vuillermoz wrote in the *Revue musical* in 1925: "There are many ways to perform Debussy, but there is only one way to play Ravel."[19] This "one way" is to perform exactly what is in the score with scrupulous attention given to reading the music from the outset. There should be strict compliance with all of Ravel's tempos, dynamics, phrasing and articulation markings as well as his interpretive indications. There can be no rhythmic or tempo distortions, and the use of rubato should be avoided unless indicated. Examples of the few times that Ravel wanted rubato are found in "Noctuelles" (*Miroirs*, measures 33 and 117) and in the second waltz of *Valses nobles et sentimentales* (measures 25 and 57), where it is so marked. Only in rare instances would he instruct a performer to play a passage or section with more freedom, such as the figuration passages in "Oiseaux tristes" (*Miroirs*) and the *cante hondo (jondo)* section of the "Alborada del gracioso" (*Miroirs*). Even in these cases the liberty is in the curve of the phrase; the overall tempo of the measure must not be lost. This does not imply that an interpretation should be rigid and inflexible, but means that there exists a great responsibility to the score that leaves no room for impetuosity. Marguerite Long reminds us:

> Music does not have a permanent existence, only an interpretation can give it life. . . . It is a prisoner of symbols and signs. . . . The right, necessarily attributed to the interpreter to express himself in the music, involves first of all submission to the wishes of the composer and to all possible indications marked in the score. However, concerning the latter, and in our time, the composers acted differently (Debussy and Ravel being as demanding as Fauré was vague), and there is a clear evolution towards precise notation and restriction of the liberties of the performer.[20]

It is also valuable to have some background as to historical events, culture, style and temperament of the French people. Such knowledge and understanding establishes a feeling for the atmosphere and environment that nurtured the man and his music.

Pianists should approach this music with imagination and sensitivity to poetic imagery, color and nuance. The ability to inject these attributes into the music, and to project them in performance with taste and refinement, will make the difference between an artistic interpretation and a mediocre one.

13 Stuckenschmidt, 224.

14 Roger Nichols, *Ravel Remembered* (New York: W. W. Norton & Company, 1987), 62.

15 Alfred Cortot, *La Musique française de piano* (Paris: Les Éditions du Rieder, 1932), 13.

16 Arbie Orenstein, *A Ravel Reader* (New York: Columbia University Press, 1990), 312.

17 Hélène Jourdan-Morhange and Vlado Perlemuter, *Ravel d'après Ravel* (Lausanne: Éditions du Cervin, 1957), 8.

18 Marguerite Long and Pierre Laumonier, *Au Piano avec Maurice Ravel*, ed. G. Billaudot (Paris: Julliard, 1971), 83.

19 Hélène Jourdan-Morange, *Ravel et nous* (Genève: Éditions du Milieu du Monde, 1945), 179.

20 Long and Laumonier, 21–22.

TECHNIQUE

There can be no art without technique,
and no technique without art.
(Marcel Marceau)

A pianist may have an enormous talent and temperament, but without considerable technical skills they will be of little or no consequence. Gabriel Fauré (1845–1924), Ravel's composition professor at the Conservatory, told his students that musicality should be based on a serious technique. There are three main faults that often surface in the realization of Ravel's piano music: 1) the absence of a varied technique; 2) the lack of a varied touch; and 3) the improper use of the pedals.

A varied technique is the well-developed use, independence and control of the fingers, hand, wrist, forearm and arm. Beyond this one should also work on a variety of articulations for staccato, legato and portato indications. In *Le Tombeau de Couperin*, extremely rapid finger passages combined with ornaments and repeated notes recall the French harpsichordists, as well as Scarlatti and Mozart. An excellent finger technique is absolutely essential to produce this clarity, precision and evenness of sound. Marguerite Long stated: "To have fingers is not an empty expression, it is with fingers that one makes music, without them one can't do anything."[21] Attention should be paid not only to the depression of a key, but also to the issue of its release. Practicing with a high finger articulation helps to develop the strength necessary to control this release. In performance, however, keep the articulation but stay close to the keys. Practice only as fast as you can play without error.

Also of note is Ravel's exploitation of the thumb. This has resulted in some unusual technical demands. Roland-Manuel wrote:

> The use of the thumb is very remarkable in the works for piano of Ravel. It is the thumb that commands, particularly in *Gaspard de la Nuit*, one of the works most characteristic of his transcendental technique.[22]

The Toccata from *Le Tombeau de Couperin* employs the thumbs of the right and left hands in a constant rhythmic alternation and also to form inner voice lines as in measures 207 and 250.

Ravel's use of light arpeggios has always played a major role in his compositions, beginning with the *Pavane pour une infante défunte* and reaching the height of imagination in "Ondine" (*Gaspard de la Nuit*). These arpeggios can envelop, ornament, or accompany the melody, especially in his aquatic and aerial works such as *Jeux d'eau*, "Une barque sur l'océan" (*Miroirs*), "Ondine," (*Gaspard de la Nuit*), "Oiseaux tristes" (*Miroirs*) and "Noctuelles" (*Miroirs*). The French pianist and composer Henri Gil-Marchex (1892–1970) says of these arpeggios:

> This kind of very light arpeggio gives the impression of a glissando, and compels the articulation of fingers and wrist to be reduced to a minimum. Still the clearness of the performance should be as pronounced as for a brilliant arpeggio.[23]

Whether an arpeggio leading to a melodic note occurs in the preceding measure or in the measure itself, it must be played exactly as Ravel wrote it. It should not interfere with the phrase or slow down the tempo or pulse. This technique, however, rarely appears in the movements of *Le Tombeau de Couperin*. The only two instances are in measures 94 and 95 of the Prélude and measure 121 of the Menuet.

The quality and color of a sound are determined by many variables. A key can be stroked, hit, pushed or dropped upon from above the keyboard with different weights and degrees of flexibility of the arm, forearm, wrist, hand and fingers. The speed of the key descent as well as whether the key is struck on the edge, middle or close to the fallboard is also a deciding factor. According to Marguerite Long:

> There are a thousand manners of attacking a note, a thousand ways of uniting it to or separating it from the neighboring notes, a thousand varieties of accents.[24]

Every pianist should have a palette of available colors. To accomplish this one must develop an ability to imagine sound in an "inner ear" and then experiment with ways of producing it. One excellent aid involves orchestrating the passage and then attempting to duplicate the color of the instrument on the piano. All of these skills are needed to project the atmosphere as well as the poetic and emotional content of the music.

The use of the damper pedal and the una corda pedal, whether alone or in combination (**2** 𝄮.), is of the utmost importance. The sostenuto pedal should never be used in this music! Ravel composed his music on an Érard piano. This instrument, like all French pianos of that era, was not equipped with this pedal. According to Perlemuter, Ravel wanted his music to be clear and was very articulate about pedaling. Nevertheless, sometimes he wanted the damper pedal depressed for long periods of time to hold bass notes. At times this can present a problem for the performer. An enormous variety of attacks and articulations, as well as careful attention to the dynamic levels, is essential to avoid confusing the harmonies. Resorting to the use of the sostenuto pedal will destroy the atmosphere of a passage. Fluttering the pedal is also an extremely helpful technique in thinning out the sound. The nature of the instrument and the characteristics of the acoustical environment are factors that will determine its use. In general, the una corda pedal can be used in all passages marked ***pp*** or ***ppp***. However, it also has a very important use as a source of color. For example, toward the end of "Scarbo" (*Gaspard de la Nuit*, measure 592), Ravel indicated *sourdine mais* ***f*** (una corda, but ***f***).

---

21 Marguerite Long, *Au Piano avec Gabriel Fauré*, ed. G. Billaudot (Paris: Julliard, 1963), 103.

22 Roland-Manuel, 151–152.

23 Henri Gil-Marchex, *Ravel's Piano Technique*, trans. Fred Rothwell, *The Musical Times* (London: December 1, 1926), 1089.

24 Long and Laumonier, 34.

Ravel as a truck driver in the military transport service during World War I

Archduke Francis Ferdinand of Austria-Hungary, heir to the Hapsburg Empire. He was struck down by Gavrilo Princip, a Serbian revolutionary, in the streets of Sarajevo, the Bosnian capital of the Austrian empire.

This assassination precipitated a bloody conflict that lasted from August 1914 until November 1918. Historians estimate that about 10 million men were killed and 20 million wounded. More than half the Frenchmen who lost their lives were between the ages of 20 and 30.

Ravel was a witness to this slaughter and was deeply shocked and moved by his experiences in the war.

> I saw a hallucinating thing: a nightmarish city, horribly deserted and mute. . . . Undoubtedly I will see things which will be more frightful and repugnant; I don't believe I will ever experience a more profound and stranger emotion than this sort of mute terror.[27]
> (Postcard, Ravel to Jean Marnold, April 1916)

Even at the height of the war Ravel continued to have strong opinions about artistic matters. In 1916 a group of prominent French writers and musicians formed The League for the Defense of French Music to ban the performance of all German and Austrian music. Ravel refused to take part in the organization and responded with a letter that addressed the ethical issues in their bylaws as well as his disagreement with them.

> But I do not believe that "the defense of our national artistic inheritance" makes it necessary to "prohibit the performance of contemporary German and Austrian works." It would actually be damaging to French composers to ignore the output of their foreign colleagues and thus to create a kind of nationalistic clan. Our art of music, being so rich, would soon degenerate and restrict itself to obsolete formulas.[28]

After the declaration of war in 1914, Ravel was determined to play an active role in the defense of his country. This was in spite of the protestations of family and friends and the fact that he was exempt from military service because of being underweight. He complained bitterly to Roland-Manuel in a letter dated October 1, 1914:

> . . . I am well aware, my dear friend, that I work for my country in composing music! At least, they kept telling me enough to convince me of it since two months; first to prevent me from presenting myself, then to console me for my failure. Nothing was prevented, and I am not consoled.[29]

Nevertheless, after being rejected by both the infantry and air force, he first did voluntary work in a hospital caring for the wounded. Later he was engaged as a truck driver in the military transport service and ultimately sent to the front at Verdun.

EVENTS

> *Without music a State cannot exist. All the disorders, all the wars that we see in the world, only occur because of the neglect to learn music. Does not war result from a lack of union among men? . . . And were all men to learn music, would not this be the means of agreeing together, and of seeing universal peace reign throughout the world?*[25]

There were two events that had a tremendous impact on Ravel during the composition of *Le Tombeau de Couperin*: the horrors of World War I and the loss of his mother. Ravel has often been accused of being cold and unfeeling. However, this probably was a mask he used to conceal the true depth of his emotions. His friend, Jacques de Zogheb, writes:

> You see, he confided in me one evening, one speaks of the hardness of my heart. It is not true. And you know it. But I am Basque. The Basques feel deeply but seldom open up and only to very few.[26]

Historians have postulated that the victory of Germany over France in the Franco-Prussian War was probably the primary cause of World War I. French resentment and hostility towards the Germans over the loss of Alsace-Lorraine, coupled with Germany's efforts to consolidate their gains by means of alliances and militarism resulted in the formation of defensive alliances, which caused tensions that were felt by the entire European community. Meanwhile, the Austro-Hungarian monarchy continued its expansion into the Balkans. This conflicted with the spirit of nationalism and desire for freedom manifested by the Slavic people and encouraged by Russia. The conflict intensified and came to a climax on June 28, 1914 with the assassination of

25 Molière, "Le Bourgeoise Gentilhomme," *Théâtre complete, Tome deuxième* (Paris: Editions Garnier Frères), 439.

26 Émile Vuillermoz et al., 172.

27 Orenstein, *Ravel: Man and Musician*, 71.

28 H. H. Stuckenschmidt, 165.

29 Roland-Manuel, 93.

The failing health of his mother was a constant worry to Ravel. She died on January 5, 1917. The love he felt for her was the deepest emotion in his life and her death was a devastating blow from which he never recovered. Because of this tragedy and continuing poor health, Ravel was in no condition to continue his efforts in the war. He was given a temporary discharge. He then retreated to the home of Madame Fernand Dreyfus, his "wartime godmother," at Lyons-la-Forêt where he completed *Le Tombeau de Couperin.*

STYLISTIC ORIGINS: THE SUITE

The forms are the clothes of musical thought.[30]
(Alfred Cortot)

The keyboard suite is an important instrumental form that originated in the Renaissance period. It consisted of a succession of contrasting dances linked by key. In the 16th century these dances came in pairs, usually a slow dance followed by a faster dance. At that time there was a distinct difference between dance music and the more sedate music played in royal courts. This difference lessened with time and finally disappeared.

In Germany, Johann Jacob Froberger (1617–67) was the precursor of J. S. Bach in the development of the suite. He established the Allemande, Courante and Sarabande as the standardized succession of movements. Toward the end of the century, the Gigue was added to Froberger's format and the suite took on the established order of four dances. Many optional dances such as the Menuet, Gavotte, Loure, Bourrée and Polonaise were also introduced at this time.

Johann Sebastian Bach (1685–1750) used this traditional sequence in his keyboard suites and Partitas: Allemande, Courante, Sarabande and Gigue. The miscellaneous dances were placed between the Sarabande and Gigue. He wrote three sets of keyboard suites, six French Suites, six English Suites and six Partitas (also known as suites). The basic difference between the English and French Suites of Bach is that the English Suites open with a big Prelude and are longer and more complex. Interestingly though, they are based on French models and therefore contain French elements such as the ornamented repeated sections in some Sarabandes.

In contrast to the established order of movements established by Froberger in Germany, the French version of the suite was called *Ordre.* It consisted of a loose collection of movements, sometimes as many as 20, that resembled the suite but did not follow the typical form. The principal composer of these works was François Couperin (1668–1733). His four books of *Ordres* for solo clavecin (harpsichord), published between 1713 and 1730, consisted of 27 suites containing over 220 pieces. Most of these were in the traditional dance forms. Many were given descriptive titles in keeping with the French love of the picturesque. Examples of these include: *Les Roseaux* (The Reeds), *Les Moissonneurs* (The Reapers), *Le Rossignol en Amour* (The Nightingale in Love). Couperin also composed 12 chamber music suites for clavier and assorted other instruments, which were called *Concerts.* The first four of these *Concerts* were known as *Concerts royaux* because they were played in the court of Louis XIV (1638–1715). These four suites served as stylistic models for Ravel when he composed *Le Tombeau de Couperin.*

Mention should also be made of George Frideric Handel (1685–1759). He wrote two sets of suites for harpsichord that were published in 1720 and 1733. Although he used many of the dances contained in the traditional Suites, he added many of the keyboard forms then in use. One of the most famous movements is the "Air and Variations" (known as the "Harmonious Blacksmith") from the Fifth Suite of the first collection.

In the 19th and 20th centuries, composers continued to write suites but did not adhere to the general form of dance movements that were linked by key. Some modern keyboard examples of the suite include Suite for Two Pianos, Op. 17 by Sergei Rachmaninoff (1873–1943), *Petite suite* (Piano Duet), *Suite Bergamasque* and *Suite pour le piano* by Claude Debussy (1862–1918), Suite, Op. 14 by Béla Bartók (1881–1945), and *Le Tombeau de Couperin* by Maurice Ravel.

ORNAMENTATION

Above all things, a prodigal use of embellishments must be avoided. Regard them as spices, which may ruin the best dish or gewgaws, which may deface the most perfect building.[31]
(Carl Philipp Emanuel Bach [1714–88])

Ornaments are defined as melodic formulas used to decorate and enhance the music. In the Baroque period these ornaments usually took the form of trills, turns, mordents, long and short appoggiaturas, and acciaccaturas. They were notated by symbols or improvised by the performer. In Germany, Hans Buchner (1483–1538) wrote many compositions for organ that are found in his *Fundamentum.* These works contain the first known ornamental symbols. They consisted of a descending stem with a loop added below the note ( ). Later in the 17th century these signs became more or less uniform. J. S. Bach wrote out a list of 13 of them in the *Clavier-Büchlein vor Wilhelm Friedemann Bach,* the music notebook devised for his eldest son, which was begun in the year 1720. However, the improvisational performance practices of the day gave the performer the option of adding ornaments, eliminating any ornaments except on a cadence, or exchanging one ornament for another.

In France, the first publication to use ornamental signs was *Les pièces de clavecin* composed by Jacques Champion de Chambonnières (1601–72). An explanatory table of ornaments and their execution was also provided. His successors emulated this practice in their publications although the symbols varied in many respects. In general, the ornamentation in these scores was completely and meticulously notated. The performer, however, in contrast to his peers in Germany, did not have the freedom to add, delete or substitute ornaments. Couperin, like Ravel, had an aversion to those who took liberties when interpreting his music and vigorously objected:

30 Alfred Cortot, *Cours d'Interprétation* (Paris: Librairie Musicale R. Legouix, 1934), 23.

31 Carl Philipp Emanuel Bach, *Essay on the True Art of Playing Keyboard Instruments* (Berlin: 1753) translated and edited by William J. Mitchell (New York: W. W. Norton & Co., Inc., 1949), 81.

> I am always surprised (after the pains I gave myself to mark the ornaments that suit my Pieces, of which I have given, incidentally, a clear enough explanation [if only it were!] in my special Treatise, known under the title of the *Art of Playing the Harpsichord*) to hear of people who treat them without respecting them. This is an unpardonable neglect, in view of the fact that it is not at all an optional matter to take such ornaments as one wishes. I declare then that my pieces must be performed as I have marked them.[32]
>
> (François Couperin)

The function of these ornaments was to embellish and heighten the expressiveness of the melody, to prolong the sound of long notes, and to provide rhythmic and harmonic interest. The character of these ornaments had to be compatible with the character of the piece. As works for the keyboard became more virtuosic, the ensuing ornamentation became more brilliant and rhythmically dynamic.

In the 19th century, ornaments were usually fully written out as part of the notation and for the most part, signs and symbols disappeared. Also, in opposition to the performance practices of the 18th century, the strict rules regarding the manner of executing ornaments became less rigid. The result was that many embellishments began before the beat. The trill, although beginning on the beat, started with the main note instead of the auxiliary note. The grace note gradually replaced the short appoggiatura, and the long appoggiatura was incorporated into the melodic line. Longer ornamentation such as scales, arpeggios and glissandos were employed. By the 20th century, all grace notes were taken before the beat unless the composer noted otherwise as Ravel did in *Le Tombeau de Couperin.* Some of Ravel's grace notes were actually written before the bar line so that they anticipated the beat rather than falling on it (see "Ondine" from *Gaspard de la Nuit*, measure 57 et al and *Jeux d'eau*, measure 18).

In his pre-World War I compositions, specifically *Miroirs* and *Gaspard de la Nuit,* Ravel used scales, arpeggios, glissandos and tremolos to ornament his melodies. However, in *Le Tombeau de Couperin*, he returned to the formulas of ornamentation as practiced in the 18th century and modeled his decorations on them. Although he departed from 18th-century tradition by starting all his trills on the principal note, he held to the practice of insisting that *"les petites notes doivent être frappée sur le temps"* (the ornaments must be struck on the beat).[33] Although they do not appear in the autograph, these instructions appear at the bottom of the first page of the Prélude, Forlane, Rigaudon and Menuet in the Durand edition. In this edition, they are presented as a footnote when the ornament first appears in the piece. A trill symbol (*tr*~~~) is used to denote the trills. All other ornaments he used, such as upper (inverted) mordents and lower mordents, were written out. A precedent for this was set by J. S. Bach who frequently spelled out shorter trill patterns as the inverted mordent in Cantata No. 208[34] (see example 1).

Example 1

The *mordent*, meaning "to bite," usually involved the alternation of the principal note with either the auxiliary note immediately below it (see example 2) or its mirror image, the auxiliary note immediately above it (see example 3). During the Baroque period the lower mordent was much more idiomatic than the upper mordent.

Example 2
Lower mordent

Example 3
Upper mordent

This upper mordent was rarely used except to avoid parallelism and in a rapid tempo when there was insufficient time to play even a short trill.[35] C.P.E. Bach introduced this ornament as *Der Schneller* (the "Snap") and described it as "my invariable notation of the short mordent in inversion, the upper tone of which is snapped, the other tones being played with a stiff finger"[36] (see example 4).

Example 4

C.P.E. Bach's term *Der Schneller* later became known as an inverted mordent, and after the Baroque period its use became common practice.

There were two kinds of acciaccatura identified in the Baroque period: the simultaneous acciaccatura (see example 5) and the passing acciaccatura (see example 6). C.P.E. Bach, however, reserved the term for the latter. He treated the simultaneous acciaccatura as "an unusual manner of performing a very short mordent."[37] A dissonant auxiliary note is struck simultaneously with the main note. The upper one is held and the lower one is released immediately. In the case of the inverted mordent, the lower note is held and the upper note is released immediately. This execution was employed less frequently and was usually reserved for use in extremely rapid passages. The term passing acciaccatura refers to a dissonant auxiliary tone (or tones) that are introduced into arpeggios and are not sustained.

Example 5
Simultaneous acciaccatura[38]

Example 6
Passing acciaccatura[39]

32 Robert Donington, *Baroque Music: Style and Performance* (New York: London, W. W. Norton & Co., 1982), 108.

33 Maurice Ravel, *Le Tombeau de Couperin* (Paris: Durand et Cie, 1918), 2, 10, 16, 20.

34 Frederick Neumann, *Ornamentation in Baroque and Post-Baroque Music* (New Jersey: Princeton University Press, 1978), 314.

35 Howard Ferguson, *Keyboard Interpretation* (London: Oxford University Press, 1975), 117.

36 Carl Philipp Emanuel Bach, 142.

37 Ibid., 127.

38 Ibid., 127.

39 Ibid., 160.

ABOUT THE MUSIC

I then finished Le Tombeau de Couperin. *The tribute addresses itself less in reality to Couperin himself than to the French music of the XVIII century.*[40]
(Maurice Ravel)

Tombeau is the French word for tomb or grave. Since the 17th century, this word has been used by composers as a kind of musical obituary commemorating the death of friends or significant composers. François Couperin wrote an homage for Jean-Baptiste Lully (1632–87) and Arcangelo Corelli (1653–1713) in the 18th century. Ravel renewed this tradition in the 20th century with *Le Tombeau de Couperin.*

This composition was originally intended to be an abstract tribute to the greatness of the French musical past. However, little by little, because of the sorrowful course of events during World War I, it became a dual tribute also honoring his friends who had given their lives in defense of France. In spite of this tragic background, the mood is not one of grief and the pieces themselves do not have a funereal character. The general title only suggests this idea. One must remember that a major part of the music had been sketched and nearly completed before the war.

On the title page of the autograph there is an illustration of a funerary urn drawn by Ravel. Beneath the title *Le Tombeau de Couperin* is Ravel's familiar monogram ( ). The succeeding pages consist of a set of six pieces in the form of a suite that is introduced by the Prélude and the Fugue in E minor. Three dance movements follow: Forlane (E minor), Rigaudon (C major), and Menuet (G major). The concluding movement is the Toccata (E minor). It was characteristic of Ravel that he would use dance forms to express the deep emotional trauma resulting from both the death of his mother and the loss of his friends who had fallen in battle.

> Copy, and if while copying, you remain yourself, that's because you have something to say.
> (Maurice Ravel)[41]

As an exercise to prepare himself for his project of composing a suite, Ravel wrote a piano transcription of a Forlane taken from one of François Couperin's *Concerts royaux.* In the music of *Le Tombeau de Couperin*, the grace, elegance and charm that characterized 18th-century classic French music is retained. It is not a pastiche, however, for Ravel has dressed his music in 20th-century clothes. The harmonic style, although more austere and linear than the rich sound textures found in *Gaspard de la Nuit* and *Miroirs*, is still unmistakably that of Ravel. The real affinity to Couperin lies in the clarity of writing, the ornamental elements, the embellishments, and his use of the Suite form.

Le Tombeau de Couperin was begun in the spring of 1914. A few months later on August 3, 1914, Germany declared war against France. The rough drafts are devoted to sketches of the Prélude, Fugue, Forlane, Menuet, and also a Bourrée, which was not used. Except for some rhythmic resemblance to the Rigaudon found in the Bourrée, there is not a trace of the Rigaudon or the Toccata in these sketches. This fact and the appearance of the initial phrase of the Trio in the middle of the drafts of the Forlane seem to indicate that he stopped work on *Le Tombeau de Couperin* to complete the Trio. This wish was expressed in a letter dated September 26, 1914 to Lucien Garban (1877–1959), a close friend and proofreader for Durand et Cie:

> In five weeks I have put in the work of five months. I wanted to finish my Trio before enlisting.[42]

The Rigaudon and the Toccata were probably written at Lyons-la-Forêt after he was discharged in 1917. A transcription of the suite for orchestra was made in 1919 without the Fugue and Toccata.

I. Prélude 16

Dedication: *in memory of First Lieutenant Jacques Charlot*
(He was a cousin of the publisher Jacques Durand. Charlot worked in Durand's publishing house and transcribed several of Ravel's works.)

The word *prélude* is derived from the medieval Latin word *praeludere*, which means "to play before." In music its classical function was to serve as an introduction to a suite or before another composition such as a fugue. In its natural evolution, Chopin made it a single independent composition, richly poetic and imaginative. His example was followed by Rachmaninoff, Scriabin and Shostakovich. Debussy brought the prélude to its highest peak of development, at the same time still retaining its basic characteristic of brevity.

Ravel's Prélude reverts to its original connotation and serves as an introduction to *Le Tombeau de Couperin.* The lean texture, perpetual motion of the triplets, fast ornaments and quality of sound establish the connection with Couperin. The Prélude should be played in a lively but not too rapid manner since the utmost clarity and articulation of the fingers is essential, but if the piece is played too slowly it loses color and becomes boring.

Ravel asked Vlado Perlemuter to be very economical in his use of the pedal.[43] In the beginning only short and shallow pedaling should be employed. The ornaments, in spite of the rapid tempo, MUST be played on the beat as indicated by Ravel in the score. Instructions for the realization of these ornaments are given in the footnotes.

---

40 Roland-Manuel, 99.

41 Hélène Jourdan-Morhange, 63.

42 Roland-Manuel, 92–93.

43 Jourdan-Morhange and Perlemuter, 63.

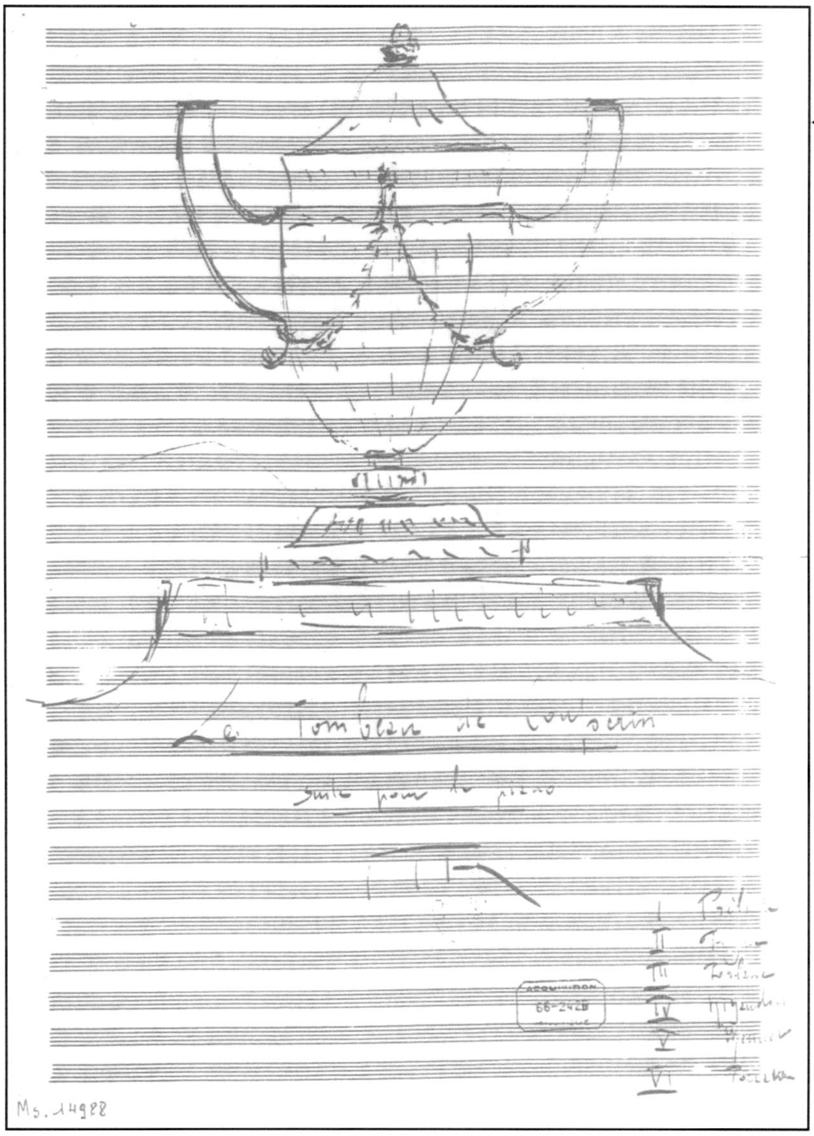

The title page of Le Tombeau de Couperin was based on this original sketch designed by Ravel.

"Fugue out of Fashion" in *Magazine of Music* (November 1885) states:

> To the average Briton the fugue is still an acute phase of a disease of dulness which occasionally breaks out in drawing rooms, and is known there as classical music.[45]

Ravel's Fugue was much maligned in the years following its publication by Durand. Many French musicians say that he only included the Fugue in *Le Tombeau de Couperin* to prove that he could write in that form. They further believed that it was composed as a reaction to compensate for his continual failures to pass the fugue competition required in the preliminary round of the *Prix de Rome* competition. While Ravel's craftsmanship is certainly evident in this piece, it is also rich in lyricism, inner intensity, and communicative content.

The three-voice fugue has a limited register and a triadic subject built on four notes that are fragmented by short phrases (see example 7).

***Example** 7*
Subject (measures 1–3)

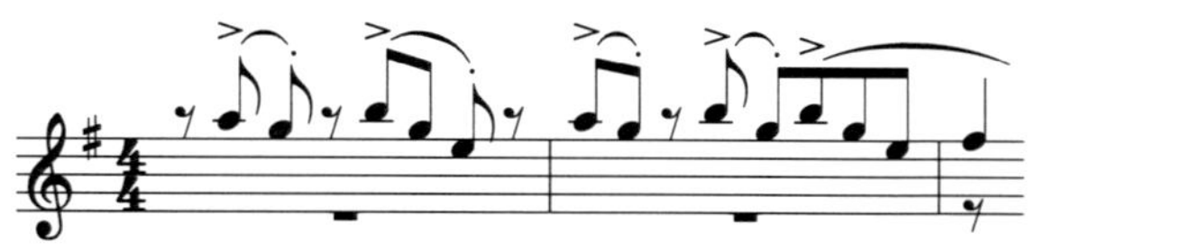

It is followed by a very expressive countersubject in the dominant (see example 8). Alfred Cortot felt that this countersubject was musically more important than the subject and serves, for the most part, as a real subject.

Example 8
Countersubject (measure 4)

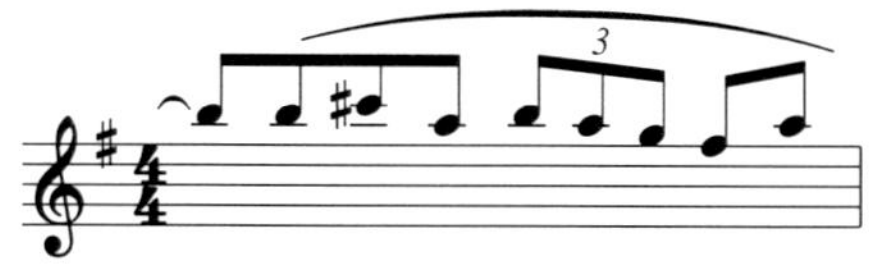

Rhythmic accents give the Fugue its character but present great challenges for the performer. They are not harsh accents but an expressive leaning on the note. These accents continue throughout the piece and demand great independence of both hands and fingers. The fingering given in this edited score may seem intricate but it facilitates the execution of the complex phrasing and accents. In general, do not emphasize the entrance of the voices. They are easily heard without added projection. This is especially important for the stretto in the brief coda that concludes the piece (see example 9). These notes should fade to the sound of the vibrations of the final chord.

II. Fugue 24

Dedication: *in memory of Second Lieutenant Jean Cruppi*
(His mother, Madame Jean Cruppi, whose husband was an influential statesman in the French government, was responsible for the first performance of Ravel's *L'Heure espagnole*.)

Fugue is derived from the Italian word *fuga*, which means flight. In psychiatry the term is used to describe a journey or flight that is associated with amnesia. In music, the term refers to a form in which a subject is stated and then imitated by a definite number of other voices in close succession. In other words, the subject takes "flight" and the other voices follow, chasing each other.

> A fugue is a piece of music in which the voices come in one after another and the audience goes out one after another.[44]
> (Anonymous)

Unfortunately, this quotation reflects the opinion of many people in Ravel's generation who regarded the fugue as some kind of scholarly discipline that must be mastered. George Bernard Shaw (1856–1950), critic and writer, in his article

44 *An Encyclopedia of Quotations About Music*, compiled by Nat Shapiro (New York: Da Capo Press, Inc., 1977), 41.

45 Ibid., 138.

Example 9

Coda (measures 58–61)

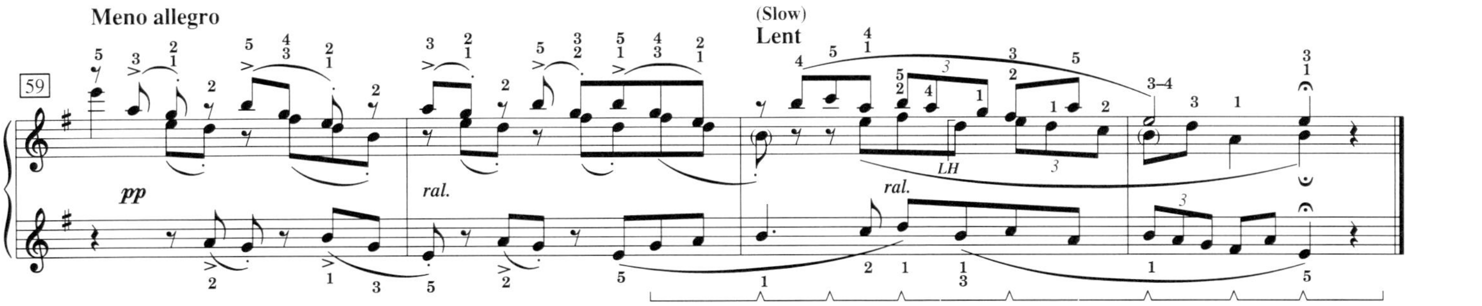

The Fugue is extremely difficult to memorize and requires the utmost concentration to perform. An incident related by Marguerite Long sheds some light on why many French pianists began the practice of playing *Le Tombeau de Couperin* without the Fugue. Ravel said to her one day:

> "I do not understand how you can play that fugue by heart and nothing happens to you!" "You had better hold your tongue," I responded sharply. Naturally, I approached the next performance with extreme apprehension and the accident took place exactly then; what nerves can do to an artist is unbelievable. I never played the Tombeau again without leaving out the Fugue. Ravel was not happy, but he preferred that cut rather than abandoning the work, which I would have certainly done, I was that unhappy.[46]

The feeling of this Fugue *is* rather elegiac and melancholy. It has an intensely expressive character and should not be played as an academic exercise.

III. Forlane. 28

Dedication: *in memory of First Lieutenant Gabriel Deluc*
(He was a friend from St.-Jean-de-Luz.)

The *Forlane (forlana)* originated in Friuli, a district of northern Italy. It was a lively folk dance of the 16th century. At the beginning of the 17th century it became popular at the public balls in Venice. From there it spread to France where it flourished as a lively and elegant court dance. Carlo de Blasis (1797–1878), ballet dancer and choreographer, gave us his reflections on the *forlana* in his *Manuel complet de la dance:*

> It is a dance that tries to picture love and pleasure. Every movement, every gesture, is made with languishing grace. Inspired by the accompaniment of the mandolins, the tambourines and the castanets, the dancing lady tries to arouse the passion of her partner by her liveliness and graceful swiftness. The two partners join, then separate, and every one of their movements tries to imitate the gestures of love, of archness and of coquetry.[47]

The Forlane was usually in compound duple meter ($\frac{6}{8}$ or $\frac{6}{4}$) with dotted rhythms, and always in Rondo form. At the time of Couperin, Telemann and Bach, the tempo was quite fast and similar to that of a Gigue. From the 18th century to the present time the Forlane often appears as part of a suite.

I believe that Ravel's Forlane is the piece in *Le Tombeau de Couperin* that most reflects his allegiance to the past. However, even though he worked within the limitations of modal harmonies, archaic cadences, and Baroque forms, he nevertheless retained his own personal identification in his melodic and harmonic realizations. For example, he compressed the entire chromatic scale into the left-hand chords in the first four measures of the piece (see example 10), with the exception of the D-natural. This D-natural appears as the last note in the right hand and serves as a modal leading tone to the E minor tonic harmony in measure 5.

---

46 Long and Laumonier, 144.

47 Paul Nettl, *The Story of Dance Music* (New York: Philosophical Library, Inc., 1947), 187.

Example 10
(measures 1–5)

The tempo should not be too slow. The pulse should be felt in two and the rhythm should have a rocking and sensual quality. Ravel insisted on taking all the repeats and the continued modality can become monotonous. To avoid this, the 16th notes should be light, easy, and never too long. The performer must consistently observe an identical tempo among the interludes and refrains. Ravel insisted that it be metronomic. The pedal should enrich the resonance of each harmony but should not interfere with the clarity of the chord progressions.

Two interesting features are found in the rough drafts of the Forlane. One is the surprising reference to the opening theme of the Trio (see example 11), which leaves one to presume that this idea was originally intended to be part of the Forlane.

Example 11
Rough draft of the Forlane, fourth leaf, back page

The other was his use of symbols to indicate ornaments (see example 12) instead of the written-out ornamentation found in the final copy.

Example 12
Rough draft of the Forlane, third leaf, front page

IV. Rigaudon 36

Dedication: *in memory of Pierre and Pascal Gaudin*
(They were the composer's childhood friends from St.-Jean-de-Luz who were killed by the same bombshell. In his youth, Ravel was inseparable from their sister Marie.)

There is much controversy as to the source of the Rigaudon. Speculation has sometimes traced its origins to sailors from the region in France known as Provence. Others, such as Jean Jacques Rousseau (1712–78), philosopher and political theorist, supported the hypothesis that its name came from a French dancing master named Rigaud, who invented the dance and introduced it to Parisian society in 1630. The Rigaudon appeared in French ballets and in the optional dances of the suite at the end of the 17th century. Jean-Philippe Rameau (1683–1764) used this dance in nearly all of his operas and it became fashionable as a court dance during the reign of Louis XV (1710–74). This rapid growth in popularity in the 18th century quickly spread to Germany, and especially England, where it was known as a Rigadoon. Nineteenth- and 20th-century composers such as Edvard Grieg (1843–1907), Edward MacDowell (1860–1908) and Camille Saint-Saëns (1835–1921) have included this dance in their compositions.

The Rigaudon was a lively folk dance performed by a couple who ran, turned, and repeated a series of jumping or hopping steps while in place. The music was written in simple duple or quadruple meter, and the tempo was quick. It closely resembled a Bourrée that Ravel originally sketched for inclusion in the suite, but discarded in favor of the Rigaudon. The opinion is held by some that this change was made because of the similarity in the sound of the last two syllables in the name *Rigaudon* and the name of his friends *Gaudin* to whom the piece is dedicated.

It is further assumed that this assonance influenced his choice of a dedicatee for this particular piece. This hypothesis has some basis in fact when one remembers Ravel's reply when asked about the "poetic" meaning of the title of his composition *Pavane pour une Infante défunte:*

> For me, I have thought, in putting together the words that make up this title, only of the pleasure of making an alliteration . . .[48]

Ravel's Rigaudon is in **ABA** form, but instead of a simple da capo in the reprise of the **A** section, there is a surprise modulation (see example 13).

Example 13
(measures 122–26)

One of the most important elements in the performance of this piece is the continuity of the rhythm. Any fluctuation in the tempo, such as a ritard or an accelerando, destroys this continuity and is in extremely bad taste. A straightforward execution of the rhythm and the melody in both the **A** and the **B** sections is essential. The sonority must vary and therefore it is extremely helpful to listen to Ravel's orchestral version. The pedal should always be used very discreetly. Overpedaling ruins the biting sound of the staccato notes in the **A** section and clouds the charm and clarity of the short phrases throughout the piece.

This piece has a provincial character and the performer should project a mood of uncomplicated joy.

48 Roland-Manuel, 35.

V. Menuet **42**

Dedication: *in memory of Jean Dreyfus*
(He was the stepson of Madame Fernand Dreyfus, Ravel's *marraine de guerre* [wartime godmother], who sent packages and letters to Ravel during his military service.)

The musicologist Curt Sachs (1881–1959) called the years between 1650 and 1750 the Age of the Menuet. The Menuet reigned supreme as an aristocratic social dance at the time of Louis XIV. In the 17th century, it moved from its place on the dance floor to become one of the optional movements of the suite. With the emergence of the Classical style in the latter part of the 18th century, it was the only Baroque dance form that did not become obsolete. The Menuet became the standard third movement of the Classical sonata and symphony and was used by composers such as Mozart and Haydn. Beethoven later replaced it with the Scherzo.

The origins of the Menuet are found in the Branle de Poitou, a former province of France. It was introduced to the French court in 1653 using the name Menuet. This name was derived from the *pas menu* (small step) that was part of the Branle and refers to the tiny steps that characterize the dance. It was usually performed in a semi-quick tempo; however, as it became more complicated, mannered, and constrained by social etiquette, it became slower.

> The minuet was performed in open couples; spectators and partners were saluted with ceremonial bows. With dainty little steps and glides, to the right and to the left, forward and backward, in quarter turns, approaching and retreating hand in hand, searching and evading, now side by side, now facing, now gliding past one another, the ancient dance play of courtship appears here in a last and almost unrecognizable stylization and refinement.[49]

The artificiality of the Menuet led to some criticism. Voltaire (1694–1778), one of the greatest 18th-century authors, compared the metaphysical philosophers of his day with the dancers of the Menuet:

> who in their elegant attire, bow and mince daintily across the room showing off their charms, rove without progressing a single step, and end up at the very spot from which they began.[50]

The Menuet is in triple time with an **ABA** form consisting of a Menuet–Trio–Menuet. The **B** section, or Trio, was really a contrasting Menuet, called Trio, because it was originally for three instruments and, according to the practice of the day, alternated with the other Menuet. In some keyboard suites, the Musette took the place of the Trio and the sequence became Menuet–Musette–Menuet.

The term *Musette* has two connotations: as a musical instrument and as a musical composition. The first refers to a type of small elegant bagpipe that was fashionable in the French court in the 17th and 18th century. This instrument had a windbag inflated by bellows with a small cylindrical double-reed chanter and four to six drones. The bags were usually covered with silk or velvet and the pipes were made of ivory. The second meaning refers to a musical composition of the 18th century. This was a slow pastoral dance that consisted of very delicate figurations played over a persistent pedal bass note or drone. Originally performed on a Musette that was accompanied by a *vielle de roue* (hurdy-gurdy), it was later played by other instruments.

The Menuet was Ravel's favorite of the old dances. He composed four menuets for the keyboard: *Menuet Antique* (1895), the Menuet in the *Sonatine* (1903–1905), *Menuet sur le nom d'Haydn* (1909), and the Menuet in *Le Tombeau de Couperin* (1914–1917). All these Menuets share similarities in their modal harmony, ornamentation and basic structure.

Ravel uses the traditional **ABA** form in the Menuet from *Le Tombeau de Couperin* but substitutes the Musette for the Trio in the **B** section. An extended Coda concludes the piece. Inverted mordents are extensively used and, as in the other pieces of *Le Tombeau de Couperin,* must be played on the beat. The Musette is composed of triadic parallel chords over pedal points that imitate the drone in its instrumental counterpart. In the reprise of the Menuet, Ravel superimposes the theme of the Menuet over the theme of the Musette. This predilection for joining themes, first presented individually, is also seen in the *Menuet Antique* (1895) where in the **B** section Ravel does the opposite and places the theme of the Trio over the theme of the Menuet.

The Menuet should be played lightly, at a moving tempo and with varied colors. A spirit of aristocratic grace and ease should characterize this dance.

VI. Toccata **49**

Dedication: *in memory of Captain Joseph de Marliave*
(Marliave wrote a book on Beethoven Quartets, with an introduction by Gabriel Fauré, which was published posthumously. Marliave's wife was the distinguished pianist and pedagogue, Marguerite Long.)

The word *toccata* comes from the Italian verb *toccare*, which means "to touch" (the keys). Originating in the 16th century, the Toccata was an important form of keyboard music that flourished during the Baroque period.

Basically, there were two types of toccatas: the free improvisational style of the German Toccata, and the Italian Étude *perpetuum mobile* style. In the German Toccata its characteristic improvisational style was eventually combined with a variety of other styles such as *virtuoso* and *fugal.* The general purpose was to display not only the resources of the instrument (mainly the organ), but also the creativity of the composer as well as the technical skills of the performer. The German Toccata reached its zenith in the works of J. S. Bach who wrote fugues with sections in the Toccata style.

The Étude *perpetuum mobile* style was developed by Alessandro Scarlatti (1660–1725). In his works one finds examples of toccatas written in a distinctly virtuoso manner as independent

49 Curt Sachs, *World History of the Dance*, trans. Bessie Schönberg (New York: London, W. W. Norton & Co., Inc., 1937).

50 *Encyclopaedia Britannica, Macropaedia, Knowledge in Depth* (Chicago/London/Toronto/Geneva/Sidney/Tokyo/Seoul/Johannesburg: Encyclopaedia Britannica, Inc., 1974), Vol. 5: 462.

pieces without fugues. This Étude model was brought back by composers such as Robert Schumann (1810–56) in the Toccata, Op. 7; Claude Debussy (1862–1918) in *Pour le piano;* Maurice Ravel (1875–1937) in *Le Tombeau de Couperin;* and Sergei Prokofiev (1891–1953) in the Toccata, Op. 11. These pieces became part of the standard piano repertoire and flourished as vehicles to display technical prowess. Carl Tausig (1841–71) revived interest in the impromptu character of the German model with his transcription for piano of the Toccata and Fugue in D Minor for Organ by J. S. Bach.

The Toccata, concluding movement of *Le Tombeau de Couperin*, is a work of intense animation that displays dazzling pianism. There is extensive use of repeated notes, alternating chords and octaves, and close synergy of the hands. It duplicates a certain number of technical difficulties that are found in "Scarbo" (*Gaspard de la Nuit*). I believe these difficulties have been overemphasized to a great extent and am in accord with Marguerite Long:

> The Toccata is particularly dear to me, because it is dedicated to the memory of my husband. It has the reputation of being difficult; one has even compared its pitfalls, which are very exaggerated, to those of "Scarbo." I find to the contrary that it is maybe in all the suite, the piece that "comes" the fastest.[51]

Most of the technical problems can be resolved with good arm technique, excellent fingering, appropriate *divisi* and by strict adherence to the specified dynamics. Performers wear themselves out playing at a dynamic level that far exceeds what is marked in the score. The majority of these indications are ***p*** and ***pp***. Also, the Toccata suffers when it is performed at an excessive speed. Although Ravel wanted it played quite fast, the clarity of the repeated notes and the conciseness of the Toccata rhythm are essential elements that must take precedence over excessive rapidity. One has to play with precision and in a tempo that does not vary (except for measures 57–69) in the slightest until the end of the piece.

There are several themes and these themes must dominate the textures above which they appear. They have an intense and expressive character that should be detached from the perpetual motion of the Toccata. The Suite comes to a brilliant conclusion in E major. Ravel said that this finish was "pure Saint-Saëns."

Acknowledgments

I am deeply grateful to the following individuals for their encouragement and expert counsel in the preparation of this edition: James Bonn, Stewart Gordon, Malcolm Hamilton and John Perry, who are Professors of Keyboard Studies, School of Music, University of Southern California, Los Angeles; Alan Smith and Kevin Fitz-Gerald, Professors of Keyboard Studies and Keyboard Collaborative Arts, School of Music, University of Southern California, Los Angeles; Constance Keene, Professor of Piano, Manhattan School of Music, New York; Arbie Orenstein, Professor of Music, Queens College-CUNY, Flushing, New York; James Hopkins, Professor of Theory and Composition, School of Music, University of Southern California, Los Angeles; pianists Robert MacSparran, Los Angeles, and Cécile Ousset, Paris, France; my students Emily Eun-Jung Cho and Kristi To Truong; Hughes Huffman, Administrative Coordinator, School of Music, University of Southern California, Los Angeles; Ann Pope and Brigid Zelaya, Los Angeles; Marianne Visser, Amsterdam, The Netherlands.

A very special thanks goes to Robert MacSparran for his commitment to excellence and his tireless and exceptional help in proofreading the music engravings; and to Sharon Aaronson, Editor, Alfred Publishing, for her inspiration, enthusiasm, expertise and extraordinary dedication in the preparation of this edition.

I also wish to express my appreciation and gratitude to J. Rigbie Turner, Mary Flagler Cary Curator of Music Manuscripts and Books, Pierpont Morgan Library, New York, New York, for providing me with photocopies of the rough drafts of *Le Tombeau de Couperin.*

Nancy Bricard, Los Angeles, 1997

51 Long and Laumonier, 146.

Le Tombeau de Couperin

I. Prélude

à la mémoire du lieutenant Jacques Charlot
(in memory of First Lieutenant Jacques Charlot)

Duration: 2:45 minutes

Maurice Ravel
(1875–1937)

ⓐ This line ‿ means to keep the damper pedal depressed, thus allowing the strings to vibrate.

ⓑ *Les petites notes doivent être frappée sur le temps* (the ornaments must be struck on the beat). Ravel's instruction applies to all ornaments in the Prélude. This ornament should be played as a simultaneous acciaccatura, i.e., almost as a second quickly rolled or broken upward toward the auxiliary note, which is released immediately (see section on Ornamentation). Execute the ornaments in measures 2, 4, 10, 12, 31, 33, 38, 40, 50, 52, 55, 58–60, 87 and 89 in the same manner. All other ornaments are played on the beat.

ⓒ Written out mordent.

ⓓ This top fingering enforces the phrasing, which is often ignored.

ⓔ Keep the chromatic movement of the left hand very legato in contrast with the articulated clarity of the right hand.

ⓕ Mordent. Because this ornament must be played on the beat, the dotted quarter note may be played with the G in the left hand. This will also occur, although with different notes, in measures 23–28 and 71–80.

ⓖ Using the thumb on the strong beats helps to maintain clarity and rhythm.

ⓗ Inverted mordent. Must be played on the beat.

ⓘ These accents are very important as they serve to sustain the consecutive fifths.

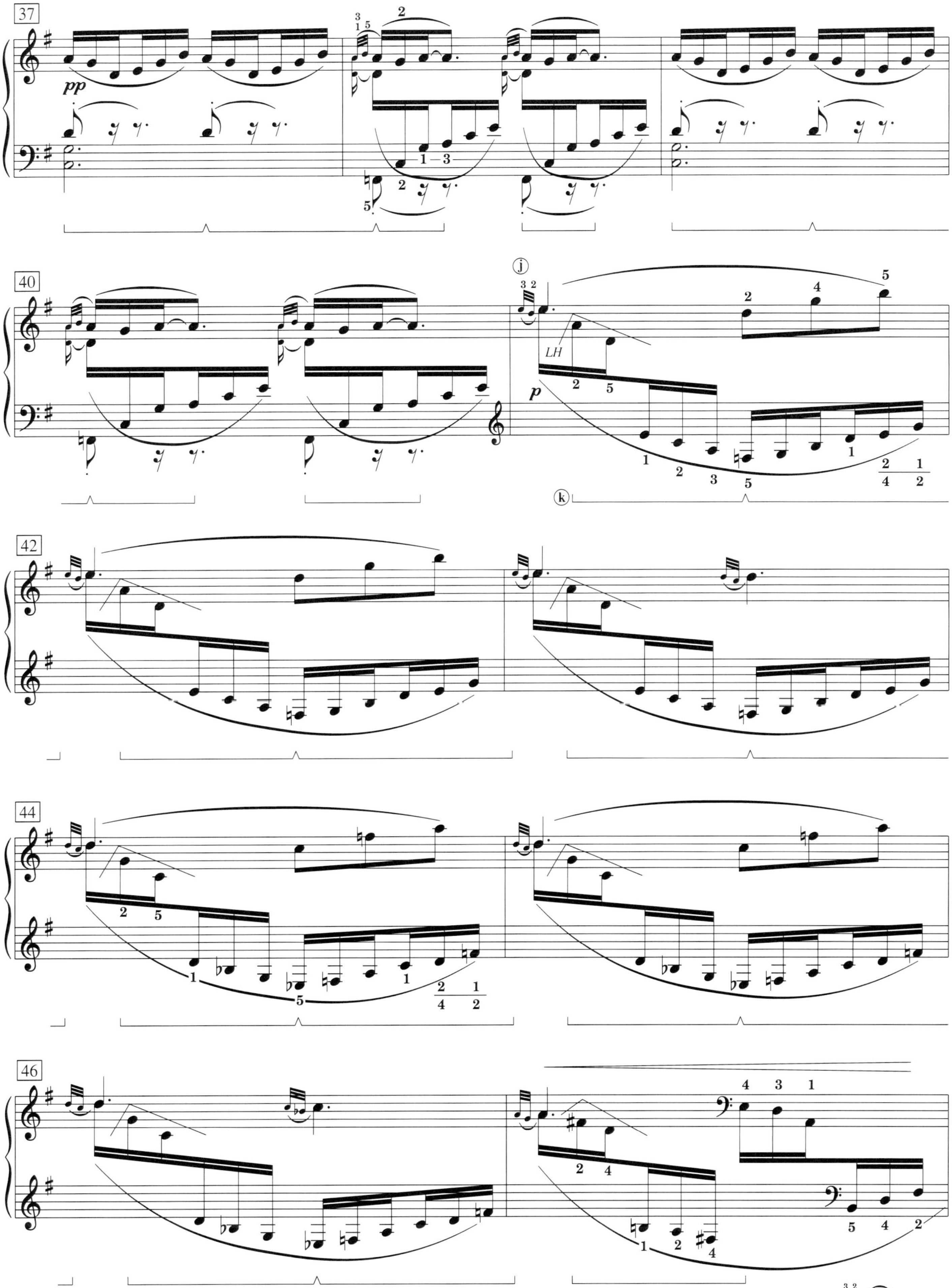

ⓙ Because this ornament must be played on the beat, the dotted quarter note E may be played with the A in the left hand. This will also occur, although with different notes, in measures 44–47, 53–54 and 56–57.

ⓚ Be careful not to depress the pedal until the sound of the auxiliary ornament has cleared in measures 41–47, 53–54 and 56–57.

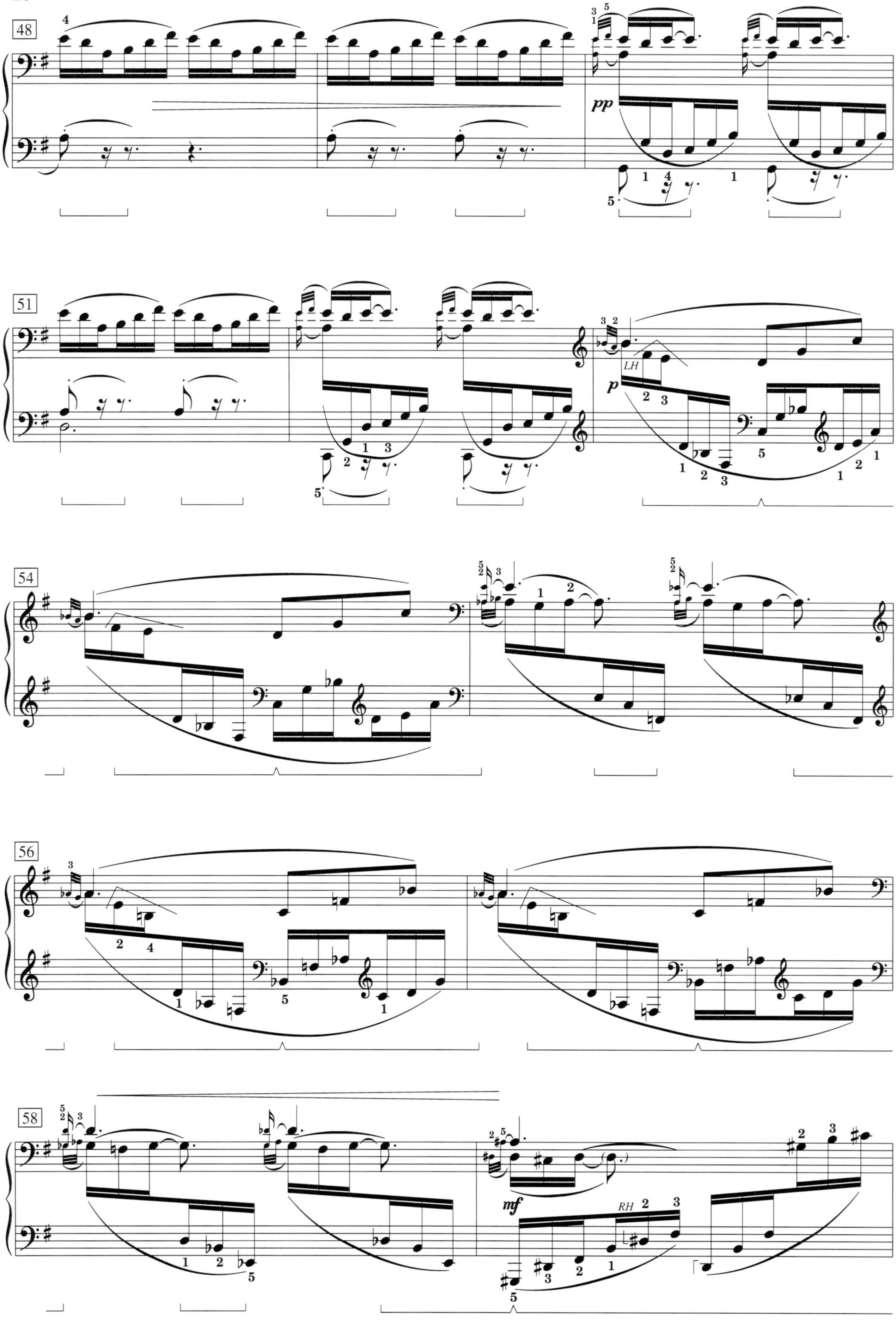
48
pp
51
p
LH
54
56
58
mf
RH

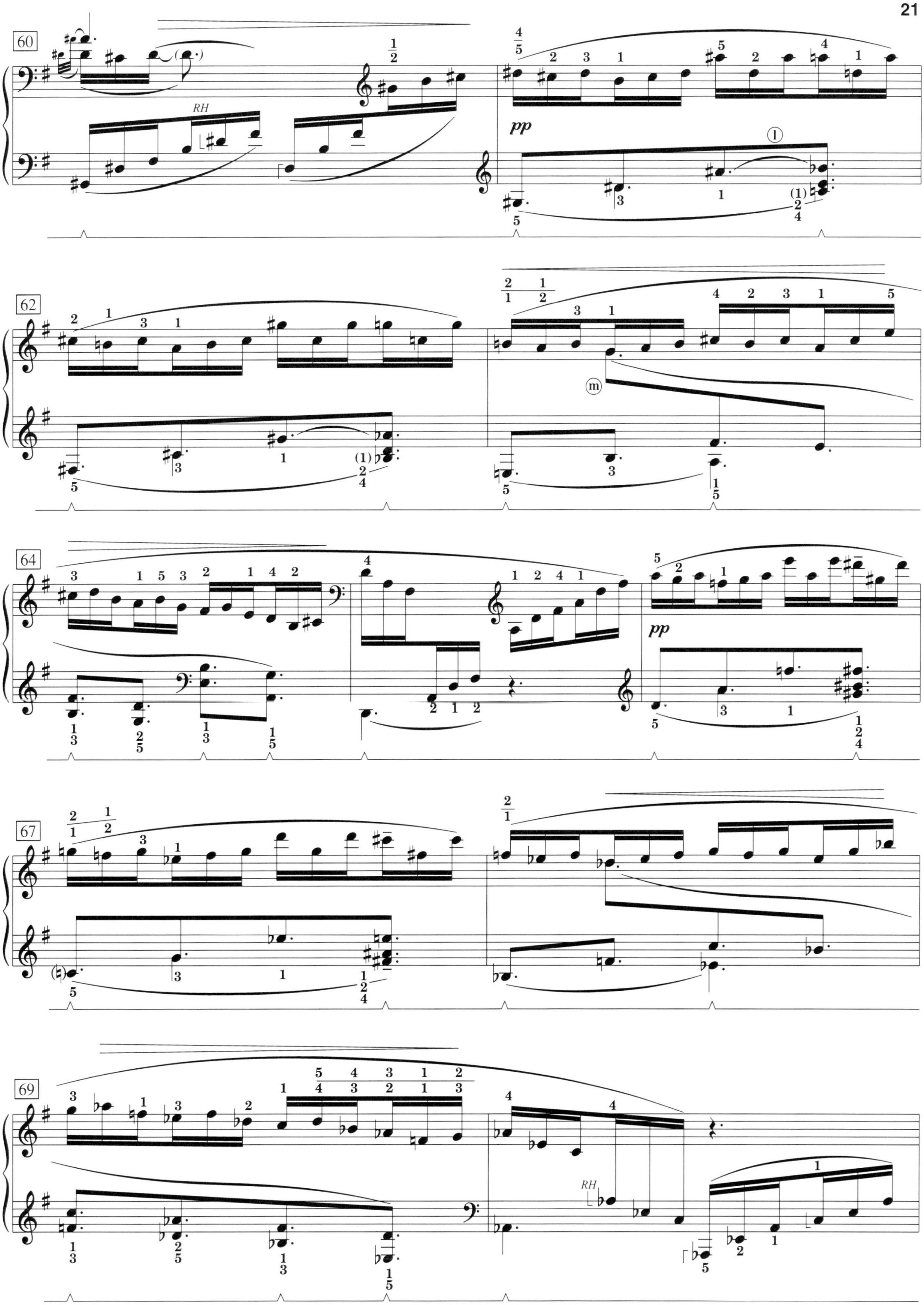

① This B-flat is enharmonically tied to the preceding A-sharp. Do not replay it.
This same principle applies to the G-sharp and A-flat in measure 62.

ⓜ Bring out this inner line.

cresc.
RH

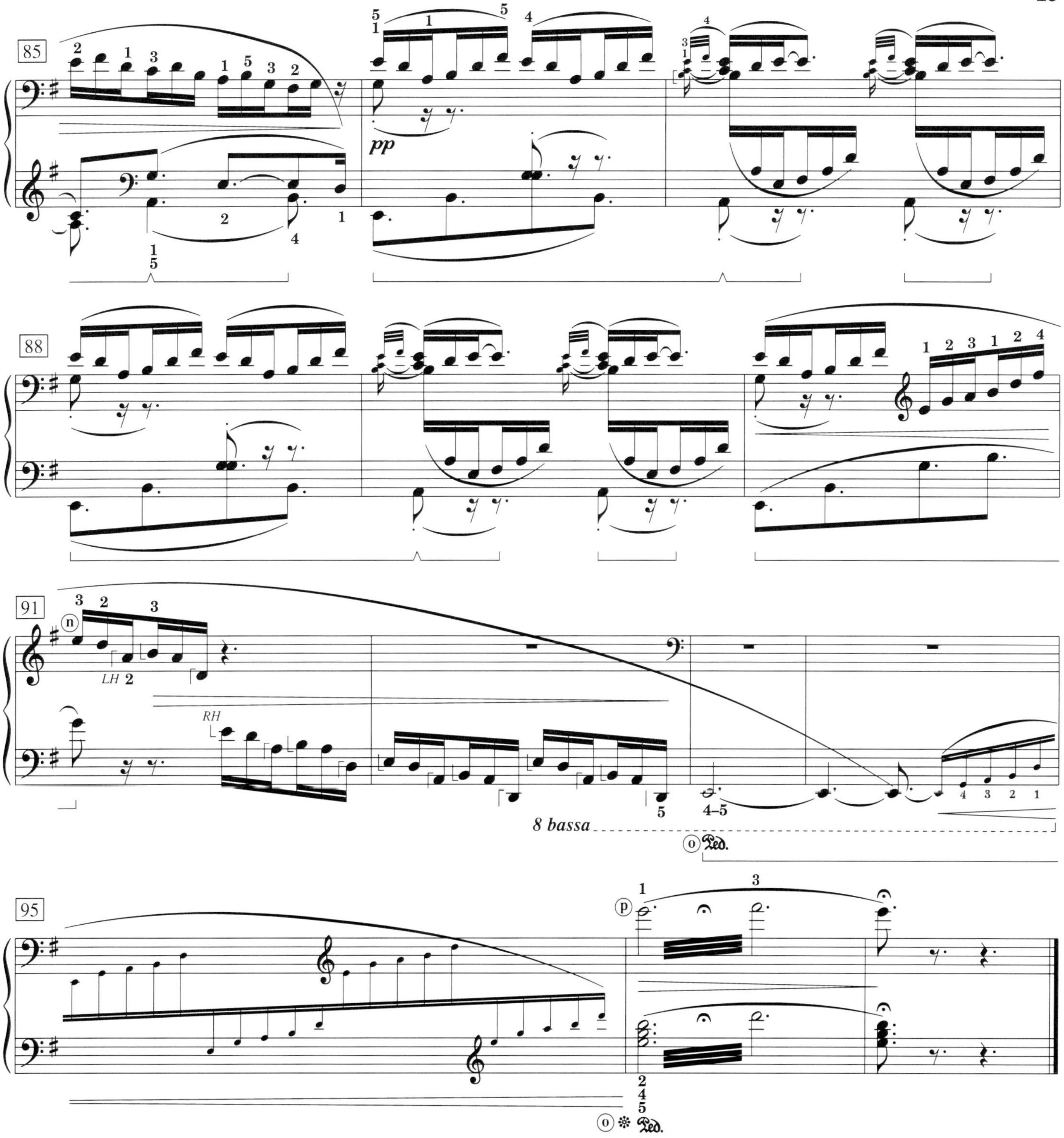

ⓝ Alternate fingerings:

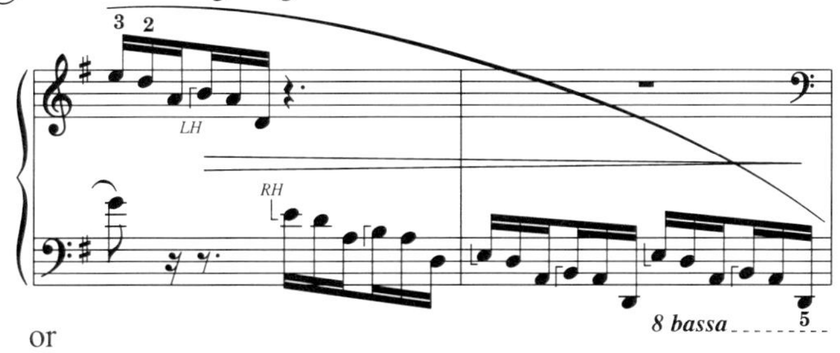

or

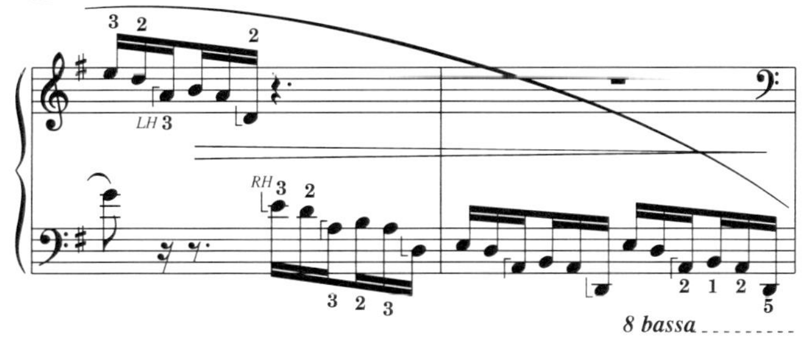

ⓞ Ravel's original pedal marks; however, he does not indicate a release at measure 97.

ⓟ Alternate fingering:

II. Fugue

à la mémoire du sous-lieutenant Jean Cruppi

(in memory of Second Lieutenant Jean Cruppi)

Duration: 3:30 minutes

Allegro moderato, ♩ = 84

ⓐ The detailed fingering in this movement facilitates the phrasing.

ⓑ Play this B with both hands so the right hand can continue to sustain the sound for the length of the measure.

ⓒ The complex harmonic textures of the Fugue make the choice of pedaling very difficult; the sound must not be dry but the pedal should be used sparingly with auditory sensitivity and the utmost discretion. The suggested way of pedaling indicated here can not take into account many important factors that must be considered such as personal touch, the instrument and the acoustics of the room. This must be left to the performer.

ⓓ Alternate fingering:

ⓔ Ravel's hand indication.

ⓕ Alternate fingering:

ⓖ This shows where Ravel's hand indications were originally placed in this measure. I find my *divisi* to be easier, so they appear in the score.

ⓗ Alternate fingering:

III. Forlane

à la mémoire du lieutenant Gabriel Deluc
(in memory of First Lieutenant Gabriel Deluc)

Duration: 5:30 minutes

ⓐ Ravel's metronome mark of ♩. = 96 is a little fast for my taste. I prefer ♩. = 88.

ⓑ This last eighth note of the group should be played lightly but must not sound like a staccato note. Take only a tiny break before the fourth beat.

ⓒ The phrasing in the ensuing five measures (5–9) has been adjusted to be consistent with the majority of similiar sections throughout this piece.

ⓓ This half-pedal change is to sustain the sound of the C-sharp and G-sharp dotted half-note interval on beat 1.

(e) These lines ‿ mean to keep the damper pedal depressed, thus allowing the strings to vibrate.

(f) Ravel's original pedal mark.

(g) *Les petites notes doivent être frappée sur le temps* (the ornaments must be struck on the beat). Ravel's instruction applies to all ornaments in the Forlane.

(h) Execute this ornament as an even 16th-note triplet and go immediately to the E. Do not pause on the preceding F-sharp.

(i) Throughout this piece, as in the Prélude, when changing the pedal, do not redepress it until the sound of the auxiliary note of the ornament has cleared.

Ⓙ This inverted mordent will push the principal note into the measure so that it is played after the beat. The chordal tones are played on the beat with the ornament.

ⓚ Alternate fingering:
This fingering is better because of the position of the hand but difficult because of the voice leading.

ⓛ The original notation shown below was changed to conform to the note values in measure 92 and the general sound and spirit of this section.

ⓜ In new reprints issued by the publisher Durand, this A-sharp notehead did not print; however, the sharp sign remained in place.

ⓝ **ERROR:** The G-sharp and C-sharp interval was erroneously written in the autograph as dotted quarter notes. The corrected dotted half notes along with the missing tenuto mark have been added here (see measure 10).

ⓞ Alternate fingering:

ⓟ Play this as an echo of the preceding passage.

ⓠ Alternate fingering:

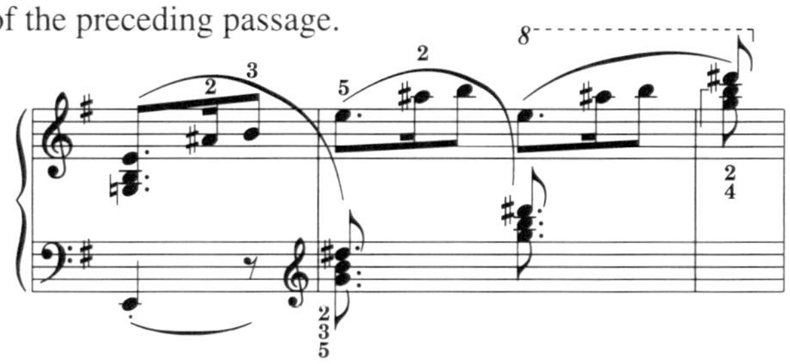

IV. Rigaudon

à la mémoire de Pierre et Pascal Gaudin

(in memory of Pierre and Pascal Gaudin)

Duration: 3:15 minutes

(a) The metronome markings in the Rigaudon are provided by the Editor. This is the only piece in *Le Tombeau de Couperin* where Ravel did not provide a metronome indication.

(b) All the 16th notes in the A section must be nonlegato.

(c) I prefer using the thumb crossing over in the left hand, so as not to turn the hand, thereby maintaining a fixed position.

(d) Ravel asked Vlado Perlemuter for a brassy sound in these passages. It is scored for trumpet in Ravel's transcription for orchestra.

(e) In new reprints issued by the publisher Durand, this B-sharp is faded to the point of being unreadable.

ⓕ Metronome marking is editorial.

ⓖ Ravel's original pedal mark.

ⓗ Maintain a consistently even bass rhythm throughout this section. In spite of the ***pp***, the melody should have a penetrating sound, similar to that of an oboe.

ⓘ *Les petites notes doivent être frappée sur le temps* (the ornaments must be struck on the beat). Ravel's instruction applies to all ornaments in the Rigaudon.

42
47
52
57
(sustained)
soutenu
62

ⓙ Ravel's original pedal mark.

ⓚ Change the color in this passage;
play with a distant and mysterious sonority.

ⓛ Alternate fingering:

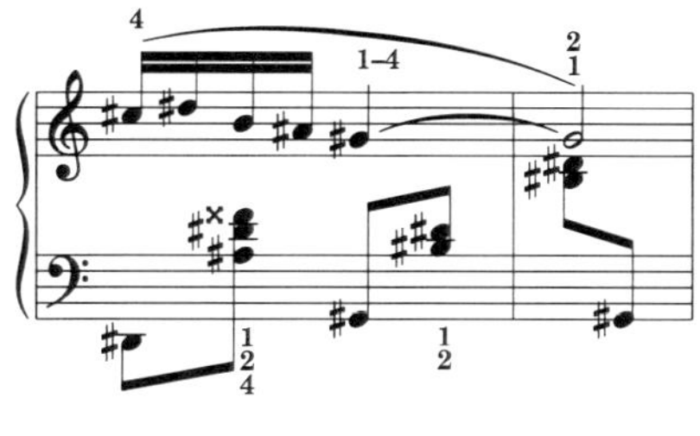

ⓜ Do not ritard these concluding measures of the B section (measures 89–92). Segue into Tempo I° without pause or break.

109
più f
113
pp
117
120
124
f
ff

V. Menuet

à la mémoire de Jean Dreyfus
(in memory of Jean Dreyfus)

Duration: 5:00 minutes

ⓐ *Les petites notes doivent être frappée sur le temps* (the ornaments must be struck on the beat). Ravel's instruction applies to all ornaments in the Menuet. The realization of this inverted mordent and other similar mordents will result in the principal notes being pushed into the measure, so that they are played after the beat. The chord notes are played on the beat with the ornament.

ⓑ Execute this ornament as an even 16th-note triplet and go directly to the E. Do not pause on the preceding G.

ⓒ Do not start the diminuendo until after this chord has been played.

ⓓ The use of the second finger is repeated to enforce this slur, which is often ignored.

ⓔ Ravel's original pedal mark.

ⓕ This first ending (measure 32) has been added by the Editor. Measure 33 originally served to accommodate both the repeat to measure 9 and the continuance into the Musette. However, this transition did not take into account the fact that, on beat 3 of measure 33, the left-hand D is not tied to the D in the left-hand chord in measure 9, and the left-hand slur in measure 33 does not extend to the left-hand B minor chord in measure 9.

ⓖ Segue into the Musette smoothly without pause or break, keeping the Musette in the same tempo as the Menuet.

ⓗ Ravel's original pedal mark.

ⓘ Ravel's original pedal mark.

(j) Ravel's original pedal mark.

(k) The use of the second finger is repeated to enforce this slur, which is often ignored.

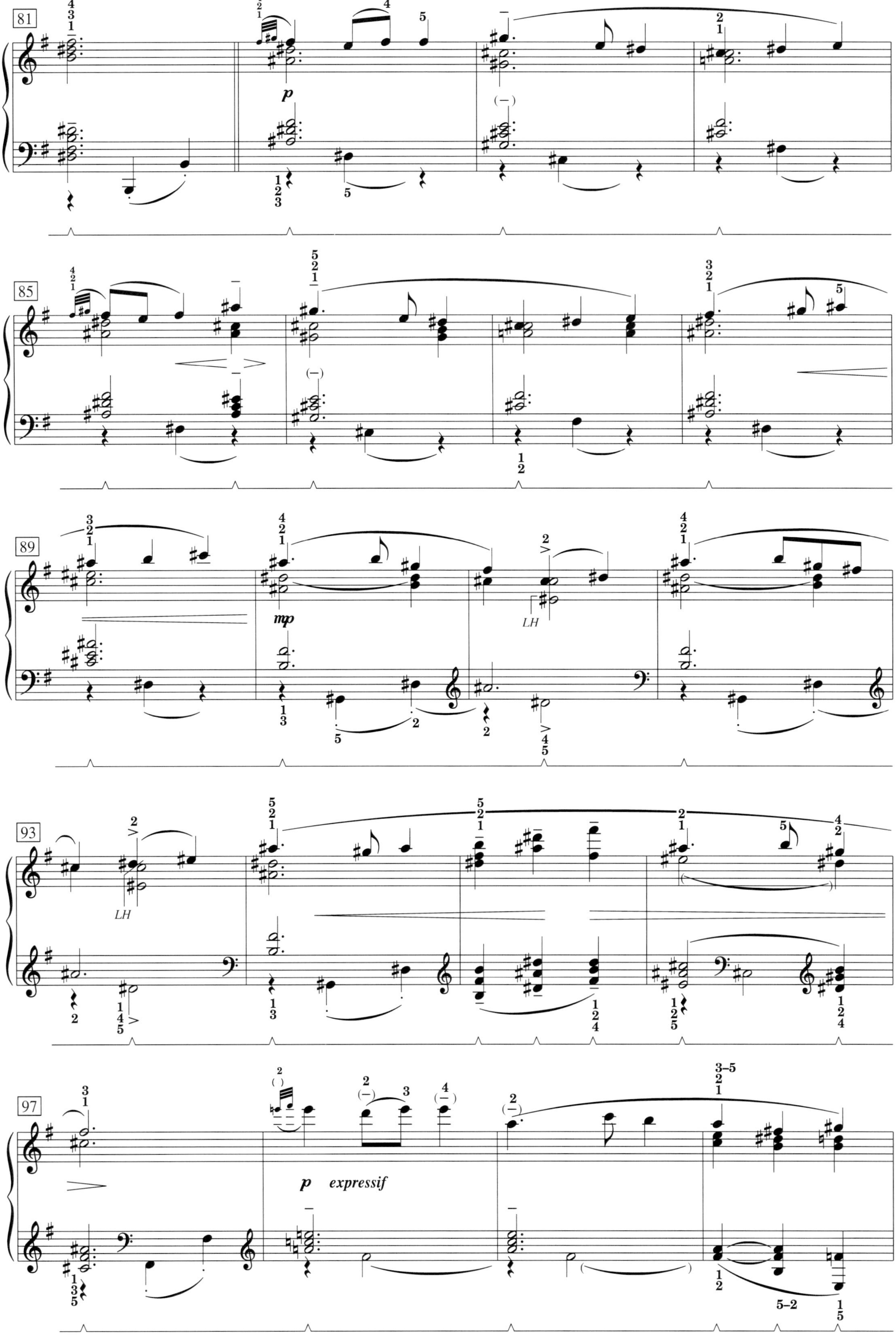
81
p
85
89
mp
LH
93
LH
97
p expressif

① Ravel's original pedal mark.

ⓜ Ravel's original pedal mark.

ⓝ These chords must be played in strict time.

ⓞ Cross the second finger of the left hand over the thumb to keep the left- and right-hand thumbs together. This ensures the greatest control in executing the trill.

ⓟ Alternate fingering: Take the B in your right hand and treat the trills as a tremolo.

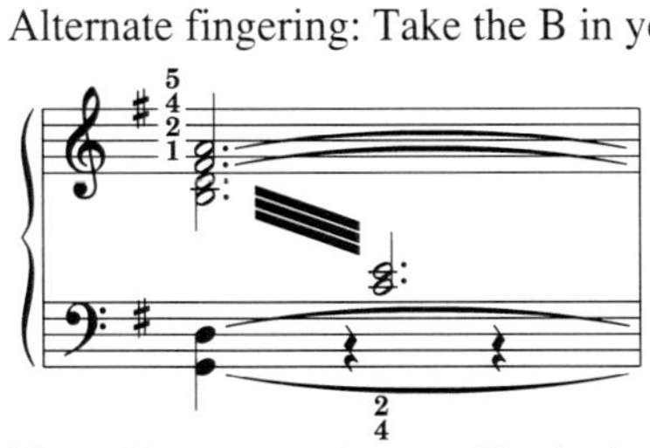

ⓠ These lines are written as "let-it-ring" slurs and not ties because of the ensuing quarter rests.

ⓡ Although this is Ravel's original pedal mark, the editor feels that it is misplaced and should be on the first beat of measure 127. If it were depressed as marked, the bass fifth with the "let-it-ring" slurs would be lost.

ⓢ Silently depress the principal trill notes B-D with the right hand so they will sound after the pedal change in measure 129.

ⓣ This *sans faire vibrer* means that the G-D fifth should not be restruck. These notes should be silently depressed, thus allowing them to sound after the pedal change in measure 129. The ties to the fifth in the last measure simply indicate Ravel's desire to have this interval heard as part of the final chord.

VI. Toccata

à la mémoire du capitaine Joseph de Marliave

(in memory of Captain Joseph de Marliave)

Duration: 4:00 minutes

(Lively)

Vif, ♩ = 144

ⓐ All 16th notes must be absolutely even throughout the piece.

ⓑ Alternate fingering:

ⓒ Alternate fingering for small hands: In beat 1, strike the right-hand G with the left hand rather than the right. In the last half of beat 2, omit the A from the right-hand chord.

ⓓ Ravel's original pedal mark.

ⓔ Alternate fingering:

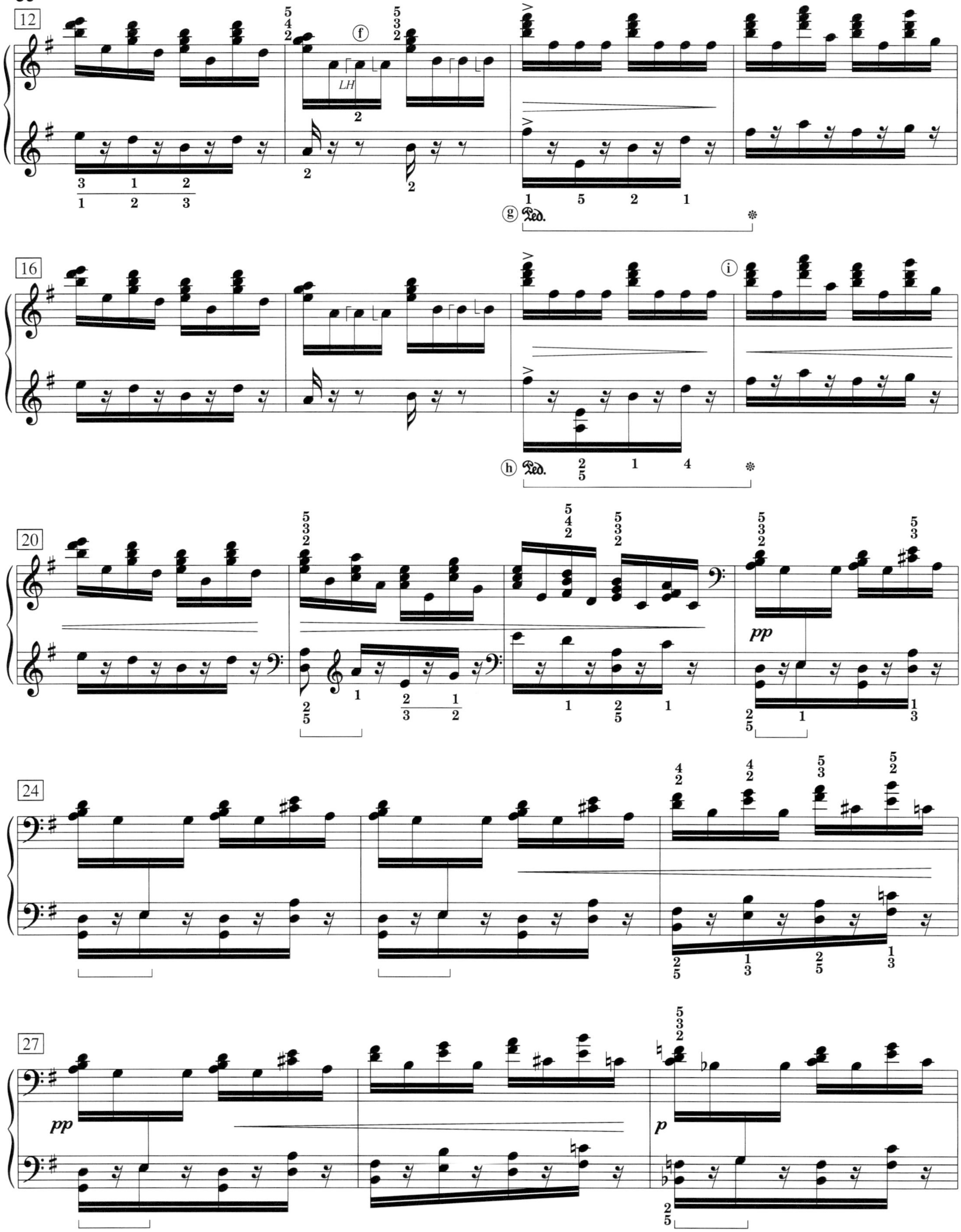

ⓕ Do not accent the repeated notes that are taken with the left hand. This applies to all similar passages involving repeated notes.

ⓖ Ravel's original pedal mark.

ⓗ Ravel's original pedal mark.

ⓘ Alternate fingering:

ⓙ Alternate fingering:

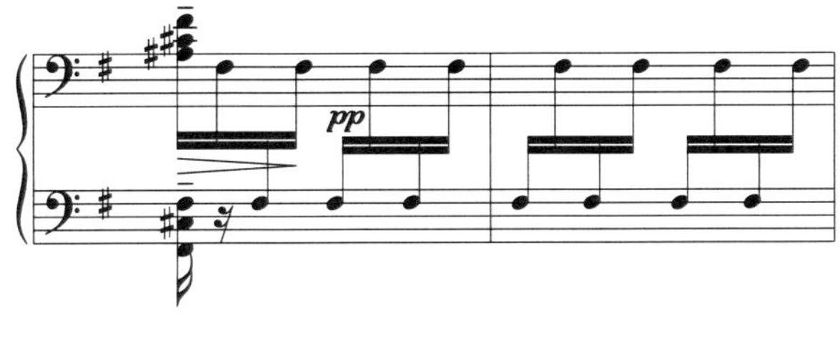

ⓚ Alternate fingering:

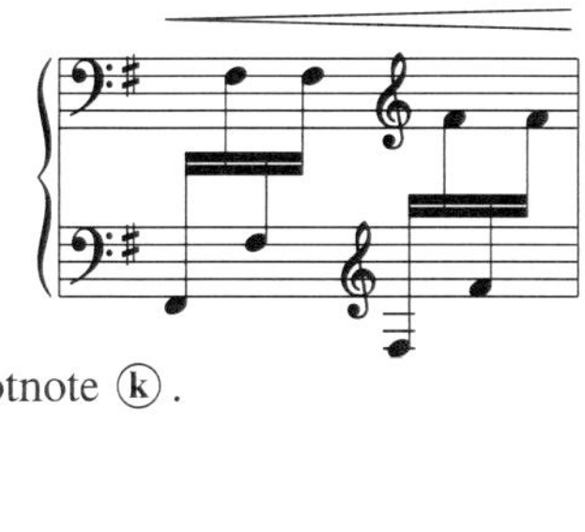

ⓛ Same *divisi* as in footnote ⓚ.

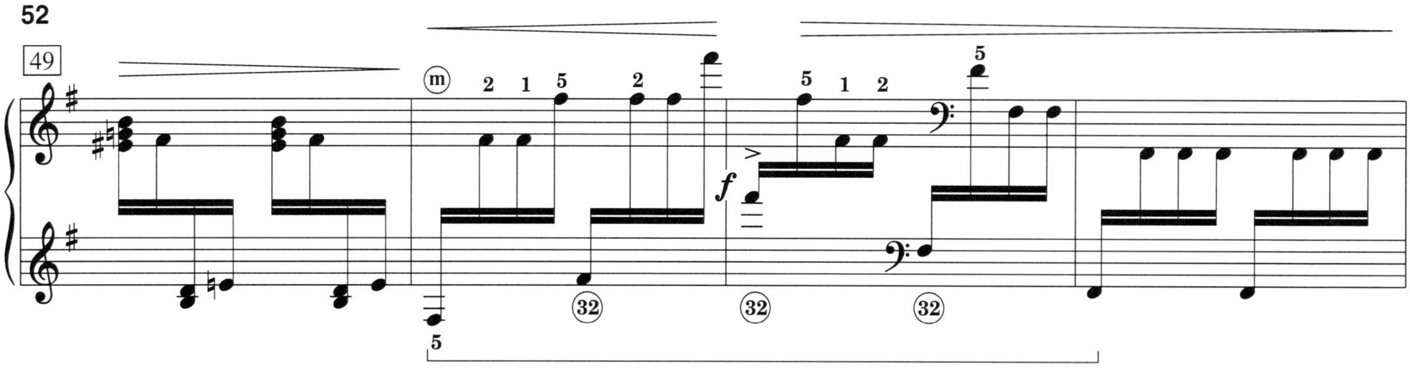

(A little less lively)

Un peu moins vif

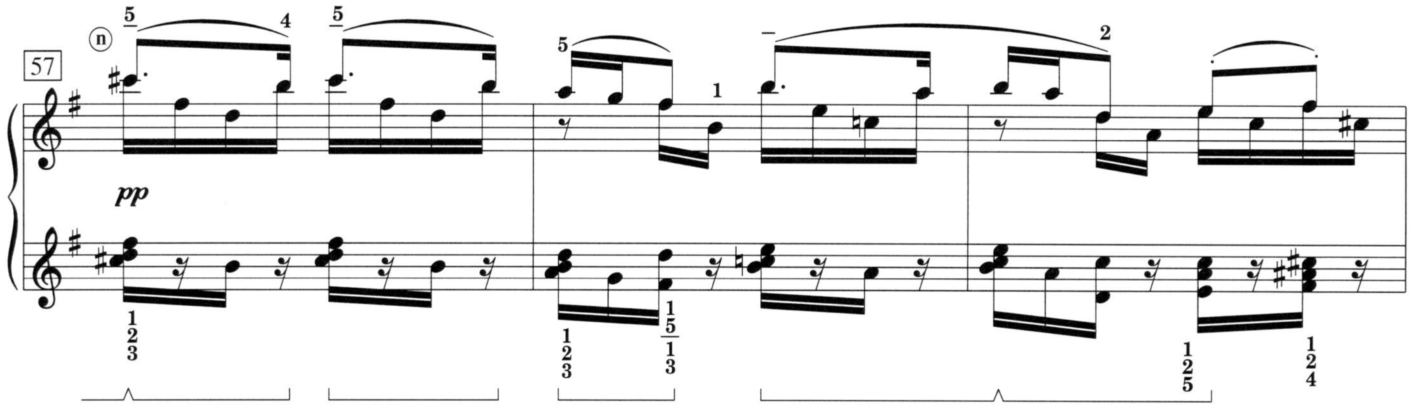

Ⓜ Alternate fingerings:

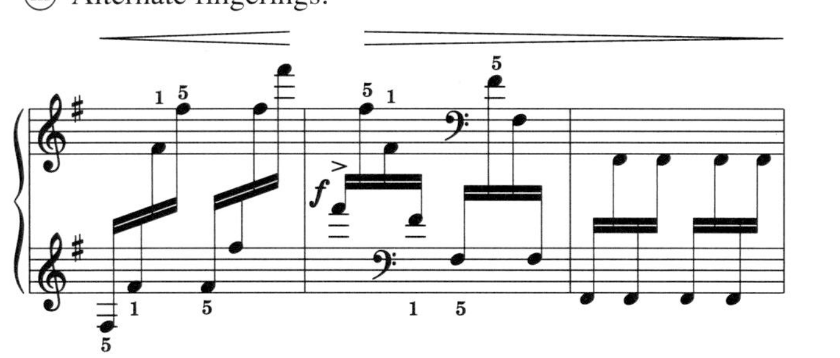

or

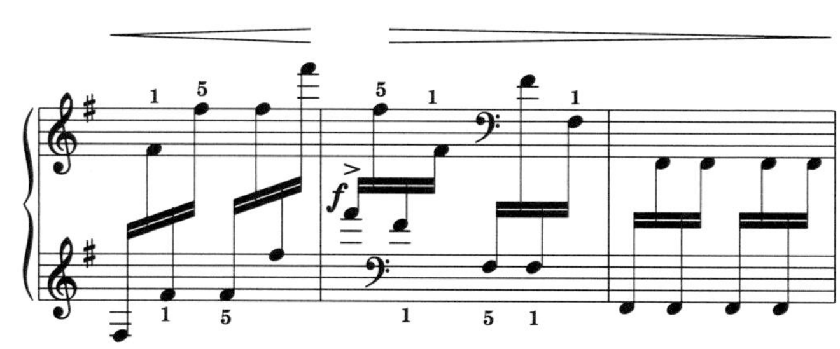

Ⓝ Play this theme very expressively with a sustained sound, keeping the character of the Toccata rhythm. Vlado Perlemuter calls it a "feverish dialogue" between the two themes.

ⓞ Alternate fingering:

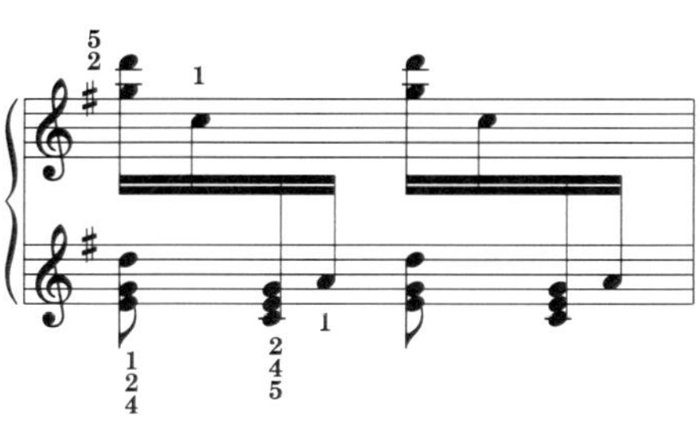

ⓟ Alternate fingering:

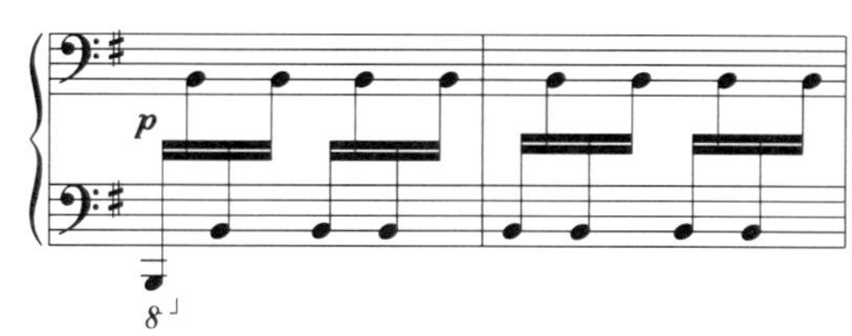

(q) According to Marguerite Long, Ravel wanted a diminuendo starting here and ending with a ***ppp*** in measure 90.

(r) Alternate fingering:

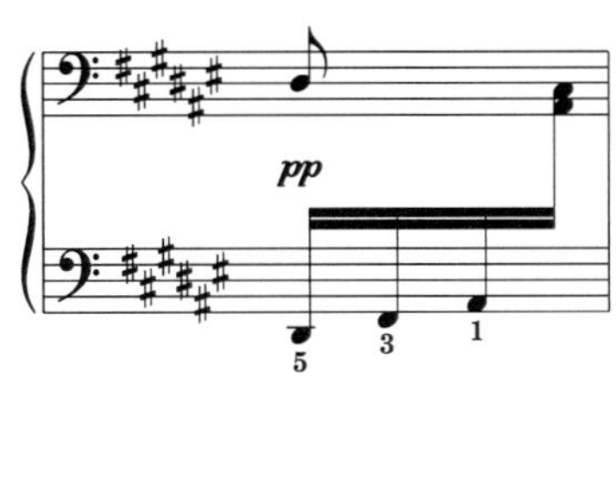

99
103
106
109
112
115

(s) **ERROR:** This E-natural appears as a G-sharp in the autograph. The editor does not believe this was Ravel's intention and has changed it to be analogous with measure 122.

(t) According to Marguerite Long, Ravel wanted a diminuendo starting here and ending with a ***ppp*** in measure 126.

(u) Alternate fingering:

(v) Play the right hand over the left hand.

Ⓦ Play the left hand over the right hand. This measure was originally written as follows:

Ⓧ Alternate fingering:

Ⓨ Ravel's original pedal mark.

ⓩ Alternate fingering:

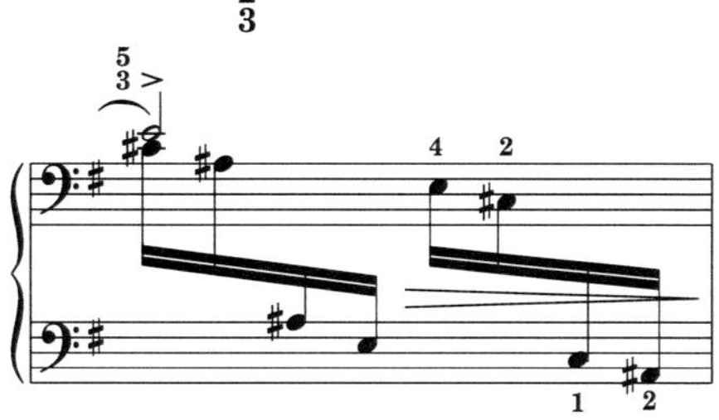

(aa) Alternate fingering:

(bb) Alternate fingering:

(cc) Ravel asked Vlado Perlemuter to use the *una corda* pedal here to prepare carefully for the crescendo beginning in measure 195. The melody should dominate.

(dd) **ERROR:** To make this chord analogous with measure 198, a sharp sign has been added in front of the A. It is not found in the autograph.

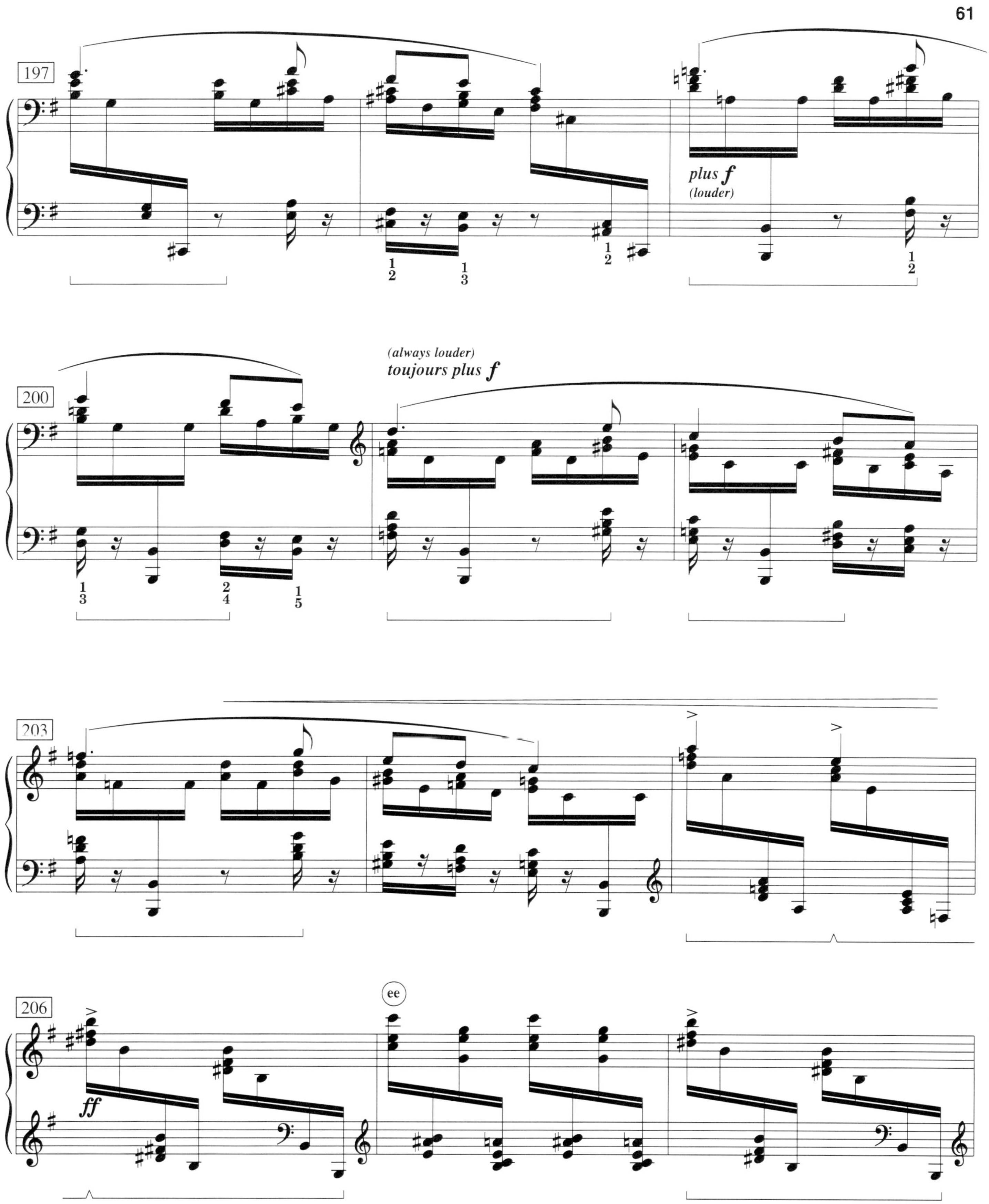

(ee) The inner notes that are played with the thumb, specifically the bottom right-hand notes and the top left-hand notes, should form a line. Match their sounds.

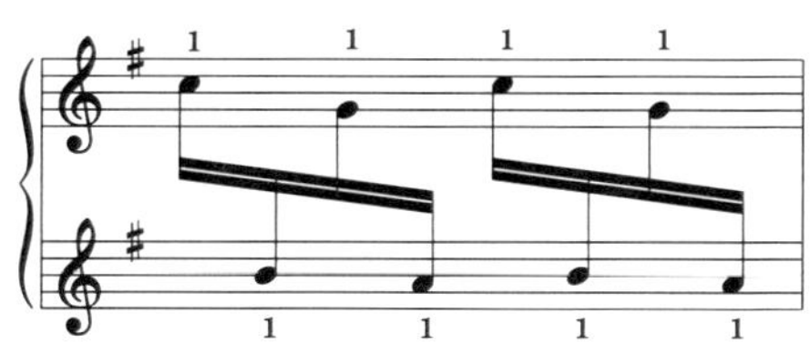

(ff) Be sure to release the pedal where marked. Observation of the fermata and rest is essential.

227
ff
230
233
235
238

Juillet 1914–Juin, Novembre 1917

July 1914–June, November 1917

(This translation is literal. It should read: July 1914, June–November 1917)

(gg) Drop the dynamic level to make a more effective crescendo.

(hh) Ravel insisted that this ending was "pure Saint-Saëns."

(ii) Note the line formed by the bottom right-hand notes and the top left-hand notes. An extremely fast roll toward the thumb can be helpful for both matching their sounds and weight stability.

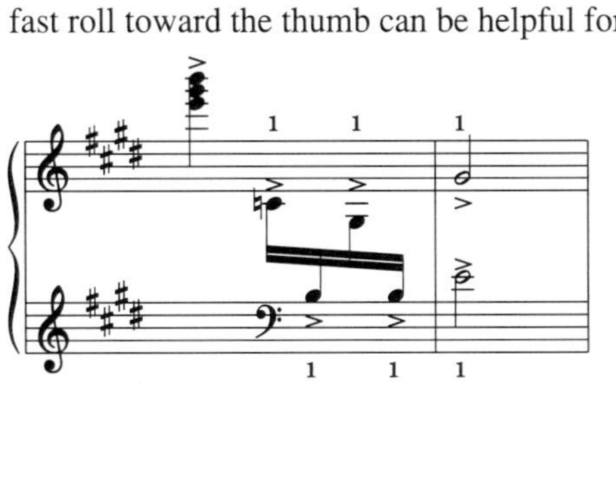